THE BARUCH PAPERS

A journal of articles to bring a timely word spoken in due season.

Introduction

Baruch was a scribe for the prophet Jeremiah. He was entrusted to write down all the words that Jeremiah received from the Lord. Baruch wrote on a scroll all the words prophesied by Jeremiah and then took the scroll with the words God spoke through Jeremiah and read them within the hearing of God's people at the temple.

There are spiritual truths and insights that God has for His people that are timely for the year 2022. They are words to encourage, teach, develop, strengthen, and prepare us for the year ahead. Enclosed in this journal are 11 articles written by men and women of God. These are articles written to bring His timely Word to those who are open and excited to hear. They are to bring life from His Word for the year ahead. It is what Proverbs 15:23 refers to as "…a word spoken in due season, how good it is."

Each journal author was free to listen to the Holy Spirit and write as the Lord led them. In this manner they are like the man for which this Journal was titled, Baruch. And, like Baruch, they have acted as a scribe by listening and then writing the Word the Lord has given them. Then, just as Baruch was instructed to read those words within the hearing of God's people, they have shared these Words with each of us.

There is no attempt to present a uniform message, only to "awaken our ears to hear as the learned" as Isaiah said. With that in mind, we are pleased and excited to present to you a timely word in due season, the season of 2022.

Special Thanks

Our thanks to our authors for seeking God for a word to share about the year to come, 2022.

Special thanks and much gratitude to our good friend, Dianne Sitter, for volunteering to edit this collection of articles for us.

May all of us seek the Holy Spirit for his personal word for us as individuals as we enter 2022.

"The law and the prophets were until John. Since that time the kingdom of God has been preached, and everyone is pressing into it." Luke 16:16 NKJV

Table of Contents

In Plain Sight

By Dianne Sitter

I love to read. Ever the romantic, I love stories set in far away lands and distant times. I am an avid fan of Christian historical fiction. My favorite stories are those that have at least three novels in a series. After all, just like in the Bible, it takes a lot of books to tell a story adequately! The stories of the persecution of the French Huguenots in the 16th century and of the Jews in WWII, the swashbuckling sword fights on pirate ships in the Caribbean, the battles for Bonnie Prince Charlie around the castles on the Scottish highland moors, the southern plantations of the American Civil War, Israel's escape from Egypt, the archeological digs in the Middle East, the Culper Ring of the American Revolutionary War; all these completely grab my interest when told in the context of people's lives who might have lived in those periods of history. I love it all: the espionage, the intrigue, the danger, the adventure, and especially, how the authors weave the characters' relationships with God into the story.

One of my favorite authors wrote three series of three books, each which were set in England about the spies of WWI. Characters from the first book reappeared in book nine! It was like meeting old friends! The last three novels of this series were about the codebreakers; men and women who worked around the clock in the Admiralty Building in London during the Great War to decode German messages. It was fascinating to me that sentences which made sense on a surface level could also have a hidden meaning which you could only understand if you could break the code. The true message was hidden in plain sight.

As I thought about those hidden, coded messages, my thoughts wandered to the people of God. I asked the Lord, "Is that me, Lord? Am I a message that is only read and understood at face value by those around me? Do people look at me and think, 'She is a nice person, a nice neighbor, with a nice family; she goes to church.'?" Is **that** my message? Is the true message I carry inside even able to be seen and heard by others, or is it hidden like in a secret code? That was a sobering thought.

Scripture says we are a letter of Christ, known and read by all men; written not with ink on tablets of stone, but by the Spirit of the living God on tablets of human hearts. (2 Cor. 3:2-3) As Christians, we carry the full deposit of God inside us. His holy Word, His Holy Spirit, His abundant life are in us, not to be kept hidden but to be revealed to all we meet. His living water and His new wine are meant to be released and flow through us in plain sight. We are to be a city on a hill, a lamp on a lampstand. The true message inside us is that not only did Jesus die to bring men forgiveness resulting in salvation and eternal life, but He was also raised from the dead to give us abundant new life in power and authority here on earth. It is called the gospel, the good news of the Kingdom. We were commissioned to take it to the nations. The real question is, have we done that?

For my part, I would have to say, "not really". I have spent most of my Christian life, close to five decades, receiving promises, fellowshipping with the saints, ministering in church, praying, worshiping, and studying the Word; safe inside the four walls. The results...new converts? The Kingdom advanced? Oh well, that is for the evangelists to do! Right?

In the beginning, God gave instructions to Adam: be fruitful and multiply; subdue the earth and rule in it. Adam was to have natural children and rule in his world. Those same instructions are for us today as well. We, His Church, are to *multiply,* not just by having natural children, but to bring into God's family new converts and disciple them. Jesus purposefully used the words ***"born** again"* when He was talking to Nicodemus. The word born was significant because it means created new/brought forth. What was true in the natural for Adam is true in the spiritual for the Church today. People who are born again are new creatures in Christ Jesus. New birth should be our focus as we advance the Kingdom and rule in it. Truthfully, I don't think I'm alone in this, but multiplication, beyond my own family, has not been evident in my walk.

The word kingdom means the king's domain, the place where he, the king, rules. Our King is Jesus. His domain is where He rules. He sits on the throne of our hearts and rules by our request and our permission. We have invited Him into our lives and submitted ourselves to Him. He also sits on the throne of Heaven, ruling the universe, and we are seated with Him there, ruling with Him. He has all authority, but He has delegated it to us, His Church, to rule in His Kingdom on earth. He chooses to rule through us. Where we go, His presence goes; His authority goes. We advance the Kingdom every time we speak forth the truth of His Word, taking new territory for His Kingdom. The increase of His government has no end. We have a role in establishing that government here on earth as it is in heaven.

Ruling in His kingdom is not what the world understands as ruling. It is not absolute control, deceptive manipulation, crushing power, or dictatorial authority. The Kingdom is not understood by the unsaved because it is paradoxical.

To prosper, you must give. To live, you must die. To be great, you must serve. If you have enemies, you must love them. We rule from a righteousness position for the good of others. We are supposed to replace the ungodliness, chaos, and hopelessness the enemy sows to the hearts of men with righteousness, peace and joy in the Holy Spirit. We are to bring righteous rule to the culture around us. We are ambassadors, government officials of truth. What we speak carries authority. The Church needs to believe that.

Unfortunately, over the years, the Church has been infiltrated with unbelief, which is none other than a kind of belief itself; a belief in what is visible, logical or reasonable apart from God. It esteems the natural realm as superior to the spiritual realm. Faith, however, is belief in the unseen, the supernatural. Faith is not just speaking the Word, but believing it will accomplish what it is sent to do. That means faith releases the supernatural. Without faith, we cannot please God.

The Church is called to be salt and light in the earth; salt for the culture, light in the darkness. Natural salt makes food more flavorful and preserves it from rapid spoilage. Jesus said that we are the salt of the earth, but when salt has become tasteless, it is good for nothing but to be thrown out and trampled underfoot by men.

Our presence in the society around us is like salt. It allows God to stay His hand in destroying it. (It was after God removed Lot that He destroyed the cities of Sodom and Gomorrah.) However, if we become tasteless, if we fail to be the Church, His presence in a fallen world, it is we who will be thrown out and trampled by men. We will be leavened instead of the other way around. We see plenty of evidence of that in the culture and in the Church today. The world's way of thinking has, in many ways, infiltrated the Church. One example of this is tolerance. The spirit of tolerance tells us that if we were truly loving people, we would accept every ungodly thing we see in society. Tolerance is not godly. It is from the enemy and has disguised itself in the Church as compassion. The Church is supposed to be the holy people of God who are the salt of the earth. God places His men and women in positions of authority in society to be salt. Their words, perspectives, beliefs, and integrity change or alter the path of ungodliness. In Scripture, Daniel, Joseph, and many others were salt in ungodly societies. Our society/government today no longer resembles its Christian roots. Where there is no salt, there **will** be decay. We have to stop shrugging our shoulders and neglecting our responsibility to be salt.

Even when we don't have an explicit position of authority in the natural, we do have a position of authority spiritually. The words we speak to those around us will affect how they think and act. All segments of our society: education, family/marriage, media, art/entertainment, business, government, are salted by our presence. Our authority and our words salt it. We are not supposed to abandon society; we are supposed to change it and govern it. Jesus said everyone will be salted with fire. For each man's work will be evident, revealed by fire, and the fire itself will test the quality of each man. (Mk. 9:49-50) If we fail to govern society, it (society/men of the world) will trample on us. We have been seeing the lack of salted authority in our nation for decades as it has redefined life, marriage, family, and gender. We have abdicated our authority over the ungodly, and they have gladly imposed their will upon our society.

In the Old Testament, God made a covenant of salt with Israel (Lev 2:13), and with David (2 Chron.13:5) Many battles were fought against heathen peoples in the Valley of Salt, the area south and east of the Dead Sea, which in Scripture is sometimes referred to as the Arabah (a sterile place, a desert). David defeated the Arameans, the Edomites, and the Moabites there. Even as far back as the time of Abraham, the War of Kings was fought in the Valley of Salt. Our battles must be fought there as well. The enemy's weapons of choice are words (He talked his way into being handed the keys here on earth.) He lies. The more he speaks a lie, the more people begin to accept it as the new truth. For example, a person may be created a man, but if he feels like a woman, he concludes he is a woman, reasoning that some people are just born that way. Such nonsense. Our weapons are also words, for there is no "new truth". There is only The Truth. Our privilege is our position of authority given to us by God when He took back the keys. We are to rule as salt.

The second thing the Church is to be is light; light in the darkness. We are to shine our light before men so that they may see our good **works** and glorify our Father in heaven. We carry the light of heaven into the darkness where the people live that Jesus died for. This is not an option; it is a mandate. *"And Jesus came up and spoke to them, saying, "All authority has been given to Me in heaven and on earth. Go therefore and make disciples of all the nations, baptizing them in the name of the Father and the Son and the Holy Spirit, teaching them to observe all that I commanded you; and lo, I am with you always, even to the end of the age."* (Mt. 28:18-20) I used to be confused by this verse, by the fact that Jesus wanted us to make disciples of the nations. I didn't understand how that could possibly happen because I was thinking the word "nation" only meant a political nation.

Genesis 12:2 God says to Abraham, *"I will make you a great nation."* The word nation is *gowy* which means person, inhabitant, populace, tribe, a people, as in the

Jewish people. Revelation 5:9-10 says that Jesus the Lamb purchased with His blood men from every tribe, tongue, people, and nation and made them to be a kingdom and priests to God that they would reign on the earth. The word nation used here is *ethnos* meaning a whole race of mankind considered as one nation as in ethnic group or as in believers. Matthew. 25:32 Jesus says the nations will be gathered before Him, and He will separate them as the shepherd separates the sheep from the goats. Again it is the word *ethnos.* 1 Peter 2:9 says we are "a chosen race, a royal priesthood, a holy nation *(ethnos),* a people for God's own possession to proclaim the excellencies of Him who has called us out of darkness into His marvelous light."

Now reading the Great Commission makes more sense to me. God's people are everywhere on the earth. His people will make disciples, each in their own cultural nation, just as we will here in our nation. However, it has always been difficult for me to begin conversations about Jesus with people I don't know. I listen to their problems, offer to pray for them, invite them to church, but to actually tell them about and introduce them to the Lord Jesus Christ; not so much. I understand we are a people set apart for His purposes; we are His light in the darkness to bring people into His Kingdom. I understand we must know Him and be His witnesses, as was His command when He left earth. I also understand there is a risk, a cost to stepping out as His witness. John Wimber said faith is spelled r-i-s-k. The good news involves much more than memorizing Bible verses. It means I have to want what God wants more than I want my own dignity. I have to care about the present condition and eternal future of others. I have to position myself so that the power of the Holy Spirit can move through me for someone else's benefit. I have to be willing to step out so people can witness that power in plain sight. Sharing the gospel should be normal. It should be natural. It should be a regular experience. In John chapter 4, Jesus shows us how to do that in the story of the woman at the well.

In this passage of Scripture, Jesus is talking with the Samaritan woman at the well. The Samaritans lived in the hill country north of Jerusalem and were descended from Jacob but were a mixed race of Jew and Assyrian with a religion containing elements of Jewish and pagan worship. The Jews didn't associate with them. In a very brief summary, Jesus is sitting by the well in Samaria when a woman comes to draw water. He begins to talk to her. He offers her living water springing up to eternal life. He exposes her sin. He explains to her that the Father is seeking true worshipers. Then He reveals who He is. His disciples have gone to get food. When they return, they are surprised He is talking to this woman. When they encourage Him to eat something, Jesus tells them He has food they don't know about. That food is to do the will and work of the

Father. Then He talks about the **harvest.**

Here is a pattern for us to witness. Jesus wasn't in the synagogue discussing the Scriptures, or with His friends at home enjoying a meal, or at a prayer meeting when He revealed who He was to this woman. (Although He was at all those places at different times in His ministry.)

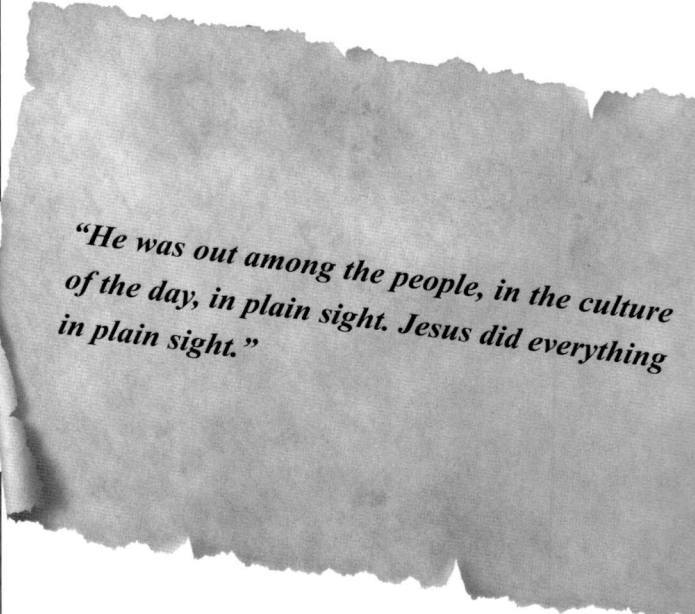

"He was out among the people, in the culture of the day, in plain sight. Jesus did everything in plain sight."

It is interesting that He was the one who started the conversation with this woman. He was intentional. We should also be intentional and initiate conversations with people we meet "on the street", out in the culture.

Jesus used an analogy that was meaningful to her at the moment. Because she had come to draw water, He used water to get her attention. Then, He offered her something supernatural, *living water.* We also need to be able to offer the unsaved something supernatural. Miraculous signs and wonders ought to follow us around wherever we go. *"For our gospel did not come to you in word only, but also in power and in the Holy Spirit and with full conviction." (1Thes.1:5)* Even Jesus said, *"If I do not do the works of My Father, do not believe Me."* (Jn. 10:37).

At the well, the Lord revealed His supernatural knowledge of the woman's past. When we witness, if we listen to the Holy Spirit, He will give us words of wisdom and knowledge, information about the people we are talking to that we couldn't possibly already know. The Holy Spirit, however, does know. *"Now we have received, not the spirit of the world, but the Spirit who is from God, so that we may know the things freely given to us by God, which things we also speak, not in words taught by human wisdom, but in those taught by the Spirit, combining spiritual thoughts with spiritual words."* (1Cor. 2:12-13) *"The secrets of his (an unbeliever) heart are disclosed; and so he will fall on his face and worship God, declaring that God is certainly among you.* (1Cor. 14:25)

Whether it is knowledge of their personal past or the demonstration of the supernatural, the result is conviction. We see how that works in Luke 5:1-11. Here we have the episode of the Lord teaching from the disciples' boat, and when He had finished, He told them to let down their nets for a catch. Peter responds by saying they had fished all night but caught nothing. However, at the Lord's bidding, they let down their nets, and two boats were filled with the fish. What was Peter's response? He fell at Jesus' feet and said, "Depart from me, for I am a sinful man." The miraculous demonstration of Jesus' power brought conviction. Does it always bring conviction? I think it does pierce the core of every man, but a hard heart of pride will not always allow it to have its purpose. We see that from the fact that the pharisees witnessed the same miracles of Jesus as the disciples, yet were threatened by them. Also, Pharaoh, who witnessed the miraculous through Moses, wasn't changed by the signs. It is not our job to convict, only to allow the power of the Holy Spirit to move through us.

Continuing with the woman at the well, she, like many of the people we encounter in the culture around us, had an incomplete concept of Messiah and of worship. Sometimes we encounter people who have heard of Jesus, but they don't **know** Him. Their thinking is flawed. Their information is inaccurate or incomplete. Sometimes we meet people who have never heard of Him. *"They who had no news of Him shall see, And they who have not heard shall understand."* (Rom. 15:21).

Not too long ago, my husband had a conversation in the airport with a young man who was from the Middle East. It was an open dialogue of what he believed and what we believed about God. This young man had heard about Jesus, but he believed He was only a prophet. My husband was able to point out his misunderstandings. This man was surprised, shocked even, that we believed God lived inside of us. While he didn't get saved at that moment, it was evident he had new things to ponder. Some sow; some water. God causes the increase.

I once tutored a young Korean girl in her home. She and her family were Buddhists. One day, an opportunity presented itself for me to pray for her non-English speaking grandmother for healing. Through a bilingual family member who translated for me, I told her that my God could heal her if she would allow me to pray for her. She didn't understand what "pray" meant, so we had

some terminology to work through. I asked her if I could touch her, and she gave me permission. She was healed within minutes of my laying hands on her, and her joy was exuberant. I was then able to share with her about the Lord. Jesus will be revealed when we step into the opportunities, He gives us.

Continuing with the story at the well, when the disciples returned, they were surprised Jesus was talking to this woman because at that point, in their relationship with Jesus, He belonged only to the Jews, not to non-Jews. Also, women were not considered equal with men. She was not someone they would have talked to. In the morning when we pray, we should ask the Lord to send us into the assignments He has prepared for us each day. Then we need to keep our eyes open and not just walk past people. To share the gospel is to be led by the Holy Spirit to bring someone to the revelation knowledge of the Savior and King. Paul says in Eph. 6:19, *"Pray on my behalf, that utterance may be given to me in the opening of my mouth, to make known with boldness the mystery of the gospel."* We should pray that same thing for ourselves each day. The will of the Father is to birth people into the Kingdom, whether they are aware of their need or not. *"And Isaiah is very bold and says,' I was found by those who did not seek Me,' I became manifest to those who did not ask for Me."* (Rom. 10:20). It is the same here and now as it was in Samaria; **people need Jesus!**

When the disciples encouraged Jesus to eat something, He told them His food was to do the will of the Father who sent Him and to accomplish His works. Then He talks about the harvest. Sometimes it is hard for me to decide which is more exciting; receiving a miracle from the Lord or being used by the Father to give one to someone else. It is so satisfying to do the work of the Father. It makes you want more and more and more. It increases your hunger for God and expands your faith.

As Jesus talked to His disciples, He said the fields were white for harvest, and the time was right to reap. The fields were ripe for harvest at the very time He was talking to His disciples! So, was He just talking about their assignment in their lifetime? We know He wasn't. The fields are always ripe for harvest. There is an old hymn, *Bringing in the Sheaves,* (1874 by Knowles Shaw). It was a song about sowing and harvesting people. Church, it is time to harvest: **Still, Yet, Again, Now, Always.** It is always time to bring people into the Kingdom of God.

At the end of the summer in 2019, while I was before the Lord, I saw in my spirit a woman, who I understood was an Israelite by her head covering. I could only see her face. She wasn't looking at me. She was looking down. That's all

I saw; then it went away. I wondered what it was all about but got no insight. The next day I saw her again, but it was as if the camera had backed up, and I could see she was doing something; she was pouring something from a small, narrow necked, clay pitcher into a larger one. Again, that was all I saw, and it left me wondering what it meant. The following day, I saw her in an even wider camera angle, and I could see that on the table in front of her, on the floor all around her and behind her on other tables, were many, many jars of all shapes and sizes. I realized then that it was the widow whom Elisha had told to go and borrow vessels from her neighbors and then pour the little bit of oil she had into them. She was then to sell it to pay her debt and prevent her children from being sold into slavery. So, being the wise woman that I am, I turned to that passage and read it and reread it, over and over. All I could see was a story of God miraculously redeeming a crisis situation. The next time I "saw" the woman, sometime soon afterward, the Lord said to me, "Dianne, how many of the vessels were filled?" And I responded, "Lord, is this a trick question?" He didn't repeat the question, He just waited for my answer. So I replied, "All of them??", hoping it was the right answer.

Within the next few days, He led me to Habakkuk 2:14 through a Spanish worship song. *"And the earth shall be filled with the knowledge of the glory of the Lord as the waters cover the sea." I kept meditating on the last part of the verse," as the waters cover the sea",* and wondered, why was it even there? The first part about the knowledge of His glory covering the earth said it all. Why did the Lord add the last part of the verse about the water covering the sea? I had just finished an article about the people of God being designed to carry His glory here on earth. So I knew the Lord wanted me to see something. As I was quiet before Him, which seemed like a long time, He asked, "Dianne, how much of the sea is covered by water?" Then I understood! , "ALL OF IT!"

The knowledge of His glory will fill the earth in the lives **of people.** In the garden, He told Adam to be fruitful and multiply. As we get closer to the end of the age, multiplication will increase. I believe He intends to use every vessel in His House. He will fill every believer with the oil of anointing. So even though I believe the Church has always had the mandate to bring in the harvest, and that there have been specific times of great revival and anointing throughout Church history, as the Holy Spirit moved in powerful ways, I believe we are about to experience an even greater one soon. I believe this will not be just for leaders or evangelists or the spiritual giants of faith. I think it will be for **all** of God's people to experience if they are willing. In the vision I saw, all the vessels in the house were filled. (Possibly, the only ones not used will be those who have a form of religion but deny the power thereof. They will choose not to be used supernaturally.) We are going to move in authority and power ushering in the fullness of His Kingdom. *"And my message and my preaching were not in persuasive words of wisdom, but in demonstration of the Spirit and of power, so that your faith would not rest on the wisdom of men, but on the power of God.* (1 Cor. 2:4-5) Signs and wonders will be released through us! It will not be housed in a single church or church group like revivals of the past. Just as in the Book of Acts where the disciples did miracles out in the open and the people watching rejoiced, resulting in their hearts being opened to hear about Jesus, it will also happen here. It will happen in public, out in the culture, in plain sight as we walk in our daily assignments.

When I look back at the many prophetic words the Lord has spoken through me in the last eight years, it is easy to see a clear theme running through them:

1. Know Who I Am.
2. Know who you are.
3. I am going to do something new that you have never seen before.

"Look among the nations! Observe! Be astonished! Wonder! Because I am doing something in your days, you would not believe if you were told. (Hab. 1:5)

I want to share with you just a small part of two of the prophecies I have given.

12/24/2017
And I would tell you there are days that are coming, a season yet ahead in which you will move out in the power and authority of My Name. From your belly will flow rivers of living water, and from your mouth will come the light of the Word. In those days, you will remember Who holds you by the power of His right hand. You will remember Who I Am. Behold, I have told you ahead of time.

02/02/2020
Hear *this Church. There is a new day dawning. It is even now breaking forth. In this new day, there is coming new manna. It is coming from heaven. You will see it, and it will satisfy your spiritual hunger. Awaken the eyes of your heart that you may see and recognize what I am doing in this new day. I am moving in the earth. I am moving in your nation. I am moving in your city. I am moving in your life. The Lord says, "Wake up! Wake Up! And see what I am doing. You won't have to say, "What is it?", for the Spirit inside of you will bear witness.*

God is about to birth something new. His Church is going

to break forth into a NEW DAY. People will be looking for answers and hope. We have the answer they need. **It is Jesus.** We have to trust the Lord and take a risk that the Holy Spirit will show up. It was the Lord who multiplied the bread and fish at the feeding of the five thousand. He did the miracle. The disciples just delivered it to the people. That's all we have to do. We just have to deliver it. Everything Jesus did was in plain sight. We have to begin to testify of Him to unbelievers. We are not living in a far away land or distant time. We are living here, in our nation, while it is still called today. *Now is the acceptable time; now is the day of salvation.* (2 Cor. 6:2) We can't keep Jesus hidden in a secret code any longer. We honor Jesus, the King, when we do the work of the Father; bringing people into the Kingdom and the Kingdom into the earth.

Dianne lives near Bowling Green, Ohio. She and her husband, Ed, have two grown sons who live in California. She is a retired Spanish teacher who continues to teach classes at BG Christian Academy.

A Quote for the Year 2022

Thomas A. Kempis was a Christian Theologian and author who served the Lord in the 1400s. He wrote a book entitled "Imitation of Christ," and his writing still has application to the hearts of believers today.

"If after being admonished once or twice, a person does not amend, do not argue with him but commit the whole matter to God that His will and honor may be furthered in all of His servants, for God knows well how to turn evil to good. Try to bear patiently with the defects and infirmities of others, whatever they may be because you also have many a fault which others must endure.

If you cannot make yourself what you would wish to be, how can you bend others to your will? We want them to be perfect, yet we do not correct our own faults. We wish them to be severely corrected, yet we will not correct ourselves. Their great liberty displeases us, yet we would not be denied what we would ask. We would have them bound by laws, yet we will allow ourselves to be restrained in nothing. Hence, it is clear how seldom we think of others as we do ourselves.

If all were perfect, what should we have to suffer from others for God's sake? But God has so ordained, that we may learn to bear with one another's burdens, for there is no man without fault, no man without burdens, no man sufficient to himself nor wise enough. Hence we must support one another, console one another, mutually help, counsel, and advise, for the measure of every man's virtue is best revealed in time of adversity – adversity that does not weaken a man but rather shows what he is."

Thomas A Kempis

A Slave to Create

By Mike Fitzpatrick

What time is it right now? Go ahead, take a look. I'll wait.

Now, what if you didn't know what time it was and you really had no easy way to find out - how would that feel to you? Would that be a freeing sensation, or would it freak you out? Many of us would choose the latter. "How will I know how long I have before I have to meet that guy for lunch?" "How much time do I have before I have to be at work?" "Do I have time to mow the yard before it gets dark outside?" Just reading those scenarios, some of you just felt your blood pressure tick up just a little. Or a lot.

What if I asked you if one day, everyone just agreed to stop? All businesses decided to close one day of the week. No one would have any errands to run. No one would have to go to work. There would be zero pressure to get all of your house projects done. There wouldn't be any sports practices to shuttle your kids to. Facebook and Instagram and Twitter and Pinterest would agree to shut down (how great would that be?). Everyone would completely understand if you didn't return their e-mail on that day because, quite frankly, they weren't checking. What if everyone decided across the board - no cheating - to take one day a week to simply stop? Would that be attractive to you?

Many of you may be too conflicted to answer that question because it simply seems too unattainable or too unrealistic to even ponder. "I don't have to go to work?" "I don't have to mow my lawn?" "I don't have to rush the kids to soccer/ballet/basketball/scouts/synchronized swimming?" We just can't wrap our minds around that, can we? So it's not worth it to even discuss. However, if I were to ask you what superpower you would want, you would be able to come up with something, even though that is simply unattainable and unrealistic (for what it's worth, the correct answer is teleportation). Why, then, can we not think about and talk about just stopping? I think it's a question that is worth pondering and doing something about.

Let's go all the way back to the beginning, shall we? In Genesis 2, we come to the tail end of the first creation narrative. It feels strange that these verses fall at the beginning of chapter 2, instead of the end of chapter one, since they put a nice bow on the initial story, but it's helpful to remember that verse and chapter breaks came long after the Bible was actually written down. Many commentators, in fact, treat these verses as if they are a part of chapter 1. In verses 1-4 we read: *"The heavens and the earth and all who live in them were completed.² On the sixth day God completed all the work that he had done, and on the seventh day God rested from all the work that he had done.³ God blessed the seventh day and made it holy, because on it God rested from all the work of creation.⁴ This is the account of the heavens and the earth when they were created.".* (CEB)

Many of you reading this article are familiar with the creation narrative, but in case not, here is a little background. In the beginning, there was God. Hard stop. Nothing else, just God. And God, in His infinite wisdom, decided to start creating.

Day One: God created the heavens and the earth. He also created light and separated it from dark. At the end of that day, He called that creation 'good.'

Day Two: God created the sky, the atmosphere. At the end of that day, He called that creation 'good.'

Day Three: God created dry land and plants. At the end of that day, He called that creation 'good.'

Day Four: God created the sun, moon, and stars. At the end of that day, He called that creation 'good.' (Are you sensing a pattern yet?)

Day Five: God created fish, sea animals, and birds. At the end of that day, He called that creation 'good.'

Day Six: God created land animals, as well as humans. At the end of that day, God looked over everything He created and called it *'very good.'*

So now that God has created everything, what is His next move? All of that - the stars, the mountains, the humans, the unicorns - is pretty hard to top. I imagine the angels (if they existed at that time) sitting on the edge of their seats, just waiting to see what God came up with next. What would He do now??

God's go-to move? He stops.

In verse 2, we read that God rested. Some might ask the question, "Did God need to rest? Was He wiped out from all that creating? If so, doesn't that mean that His omnipotence was limited?" This is one of those types of questions that theology students like to debate, but I think it bears very little significance on our lives. Perhaps a better translation of that word is 'ceased.' God, after speaking everything into existence, now ceases from His work. He stops.

Could God have created more? I think so. Did He lack the creativity to come up with new and exciting things? I don't think so. I think God made a conscious decision to stop.

God took this day, a whole day, to simply stop. He created billions upon billions of stars and planets and such in a day. He could have fit a lot more into His day than to simply stop, couldn't He? He created all of the land animals in a single day. Couldn't He have made more cool stuff and then taken a break? Probably, but He chose not to do that. Instead, He chooses to stop.

However, He wasn't done. Remember how He declared that everything He had made was good and that the entirety of His creation was very good? He didn't call what He created on this seventh day good, because He didn't create anything. However, God did have a little something to say about this day. In verse 3, we read that *"God blessed the seventh day and made it **holy**."* Everything He created is good, but when He stopped, when He ceased from creating, that's the day He said is holy. And we are told that it is called that specifically because it was when He chose to stop.

Rabbi Abraham Joshua Heschel has this to say about this verse: "In the Bible, no thing or place is holy by itself; not even the Promised Land is called holy. While the holiness of the land and of festivals depends on the actions of the Jewish people, who have to sanctify them, the holiness of the Sabbath, he writes, preceded the holiness of Israel. Even if people fail to observe the Sabbath, it remains holy."

When we toss around churchy words like 'holy,' what are we talking about? We talk about God being holy, God's people being holy, so what does it mean that something - in particular this day - is 'holy'? In the Hebrew language, holiness designates something that is separate from the ordinary or profane. In other words, something that is 'holy' is special, is distinct from anything that may be similar. When we read the word 'holy' in Scripture, there is also an implied connection to God and the divine, so to be holy means 'to be set apart for the purposes of God.' God is saying, by stopping and calling this one day of the week 'holy,' that it is a day that is set apart for the purposes of God. This day that many of us treat no differently than any other, God says it is special to Him. And this is the day that comes to be known as the Sabbath (which simply comes from a Hebrew word that means to cease, to end, or to rest).

Now, lest you think that this idea of one day a week, when God stops His work and calls it holy, is unique to God and has no bearing on our lives, particularly to those of us who function in 21st century America where *nothing stops,* let's look at a couple more passages, the first one being the

Ten Commandments. Some folks cringe when they hear 'commandment.' It can lend credence to the arguments of some that christianity is nothing more than a list of rules. I like to think about the Ten Commandments as the ways that life works best: if you follow these words, life will work best for you. Are they commandments? Yes, but they are commandments because God, since He created life, knows how life works best and wants what's best for you because of His great love for you. I mean, we give instructions to our kids because we know how life works best and want what's best for them, right? "Don't play in the street." To our kids, it may feel like we are trying to ruin their fun, but we simply want them to live. Does He give commands to ruin our fun? Of course not. He gives commands because He loves us, and the one I want to focus on is no different.

The Ten Commandments, or Ten Words, as some refer to them, appear in two different locations, Ex. 20 and Deut. 5. Space does not permit us to look at all of the commandments, but if we could, I think one thing would be very clear: the importance of this commandment that focuses on the Sabbath. According to Matthew Sleeth, "If the Ten Commandments were written on apple pie and you get to choose which slice to have based upon the size, choose the fourth [the one about the Sabbath]. You will get more than a third of the pie to put on your plate." In the CEB, 98 words are dedicated to this one commandment. The next closest is not making idols for yourself, which is comprised of 85 words. Murder, which many of us would consider one of the worst transgressions, requires only three words to communicate. Not stealing? Three words. Not committing adultery? That gets a whopping four words. Lying gets seven words. The fact that this one commandment about taking a Sabbath gets this much text dedicated to it should communicate to you and me that this is a big deal in God's mind.

As mentioned, the Ten Commandments can be found in two separate locations. It may be helpful to look at them side-by-side to discuss them further:
(see next page for the comparison)

It's fascinating that the same author, who penned both of these accounts, gave two different rationales for why the Sabbath should be recognized and set apart. In Exodus, he hearkens back to the creation account and reminds the readers that God set the Sabbath day aside as holy because that was the day that He ceased working, and because He set the pattern in place, they should go and do likewise. But then, in Deuteronomy, He assigns a completely different rationale: a means to remember that it was God who had rescued them out of slavery in Egypt. Perhaps this was due to the fact that between version 1 and version 2, the Jews had fallen into idol worship, and He wanted to make it very clear that God was the one who had rescued them from slavery in Egypt, not any of their false idols. Or perhaps He wanted them to be very clear about the fact that the Jews themselves could not claim any credit for them being saved from slavery, and because they could do nothing about it, they can now simply trust in God on the Sabbath. Regardless of why the rationale changed, what do we do with the fact that there are two rationales given? How do we make sense of that? Is one more important in some way than the other? Does one supersede the other?

What if the two are connected?

Pause for a moment to take a look at your life. If I were to ask you, "How are you?" many of you would respond with "Busy!" or something similar. Our busyness is something we often wear like a badge of honor.

Years ago, when I was between colleges, I was working at a radio station. This was one of my favorite jobs ever. At one particular point in time, I was on-air six evenings a week and loved it. During this same period of time, some friends of mine from college started getting married, and since I was a DJ, they started asking me to DJ their wedding receptions. I desperately needed the money, so I said yes every time. As a result, there was a stretch that I worked for 48 straight days without a day off. I'll tell you what, I made sure everyone knew about it, too! "How are you?" "Tired!" "Why are you so tired?" "Well, I've been working for 48 STRAIGHT DAYS!!"

We live in a culture that values the busy and the stressed. According to the Bureau of Labor Statistics, in 1969, the average young, married couple worked 56 hours/week. Thirty years later, that number had risen to 67 hours and has continued to rise since. That's the world that you and I live in.

It's not only work in the marketplace, either, is it? When we are not at our jobs, are we content to simply stop and rest? Or do we feel the need to fill up that time with other stuff, such as home projects, extracurricular activities for the kids, errands, and so on? Many of you reading this have a long to-do list on your phones, which turns your days off into 'what can I get done?' days.

Speaking of our phones, don't they make life easy? They make it so easy to connect quickly with whomever and to do whatever we need them to do. Our phones make it so that we are accessible 24/7. I read recently that the average e-mail is responded to in 90 minutes, while the average text message is responded to in 90 seconds (side note: I think I'm much faster than that). It's almost as if we don't feel like we have time to just let that issue or that text message sit for a while. We feel the pressure to tend to it and to solve it now! Rabbi Heschel had this to say about our relationship with time: "Time to us is sarcasm, a slick treacherous monster with a jaw like a furnace incinerating every moment of our lives."

When we work as much as we work, and when we fill our spare time with work and fill our mental space with e-mails and text messages and Facebook and Pinterest, when do we simply stop and rest? When do we, as God did, cease? Where is the margin in our lives?

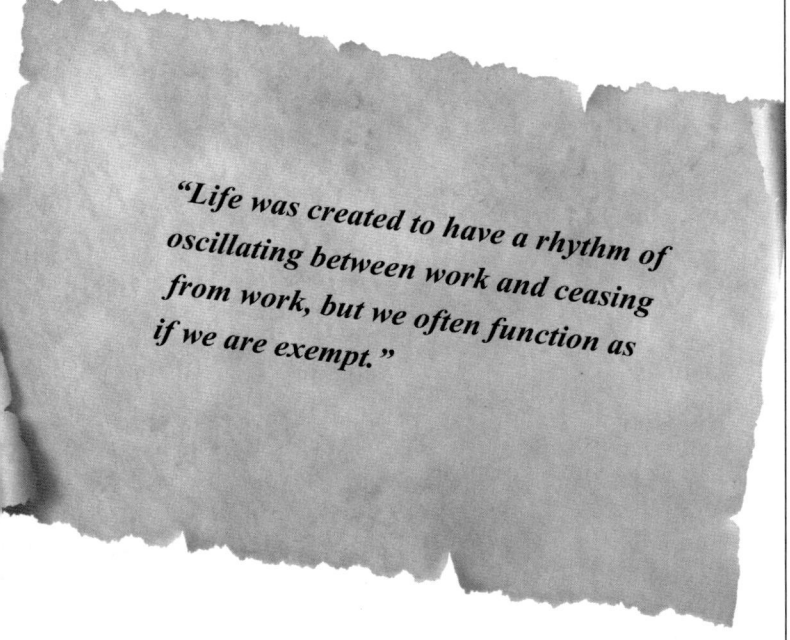

"Life was created to have a rhythm of oscillating between work and ceasing from work, but we often function as if we are exempt."

We have allowed culture to creep in to dictate how busy we should be, and so we fill our time with work, and we figure that we will cease when we retire, but that was not the pattern that God had in mind.

It's not just the fault of culture. In the beginning, we are told that we were created in God's image. I believe that part of that image is that we were created to create. God was creative and productive, and we are made in that image. We also read in the early pages of the Bible that mankind was created with work to do, so that is in our DNA. Work is not a bad thing in and of itself. However, when we take that theological truth - we were created to create and do work - and combine it with what culture tells us to do - fill every spare moment with work and busyness - the end result is being busy and getting very little rest. This has led us to a place of being enslaved by the need to create. Culture has defined what mold to fit into, and our theology, when reading the right - or wrong - way, encourages that mold. That combination ends up being a form of slavery that dictates everything about us - we have to do more, create more, be more busy. It defines who we are, it becomes our identity, and it's a bondage from which we can't break free.

My guess is that, when we are lying on our deathbed, assuming we get that opportunity, none of us will say, "Man, I wish I had spent more time at the office! If only I had gotten a few more home projects done. I just wish I had

spent a few more hours every day answering e-mails and death-scrolling on Facebook." And yet, we live every day, every week as if it were true: If I don't finish this project, if I don't do this thing in the yard, if I don't get to read through the rants on Twitter, I just won't be satisfied. That, my friends, is a form of slavery.

God is a God of freedom. He freed his children from slavery in Egypt. He freed the woman caught in adultery from the judgmental stares of her accusers. He freed the man born blind from a lifetime of darkness. He freed all of us from sin and death through the death and resurrection of Jesus. His great desire is to free you from anything that is keeping you from living the full and abundant life. He wants you to be free, not enslaved. It is my belief that the Sabbath was established by God as a gift - Jesus says that it was created FOR us - that frees us from the slavery of having to create.

Do you remember the two versions of the Sabbath commandment? If not, take a second to go back to review them. I'll wait... The version in Exodus hearkened back to Creation, while the version in Deuteronomy referenced the deliverance from slavery in Egypt. What if there is a portion of both of those rationales that God wants to use to speak to us and our view of work and rest today? On the one hand, God is saying, "Remember the Sabbath because I created everything in six days and stopped on the seventh day. You should do the same." On the other hand, He is saying, "Remember the Sabbath because I was the one who freed you from slavery. I want you to be free again." I believe that God wants you and I to be free from the slavery of 'I must do more,' free from the slavery of 'I must create more,' free from the slavery of 'I must be busy to prove my worth.'

You may be reading this article thinking that I just don't get it. You're a busy dude or dudette, and you have a lot of plates that you need to keep spinning. In that, you are right. I don't know your schedule, and I don't know your obligations. I don't know your plates. However, God does, and He had the job of creating the universe, and HE made the intentional decision to stop creating for one day out of the week. Are we saying that our job responsibilities are more pressing than His, that we have more plates to spin than God?? There's a certain amount of arrogance when we think that, consciously or unconsciously, something will fall apart if we don't take care of this right now, today. God trusted the universe to keep going on that day He rested, but somehow it will stop if we take one day off? As Sleeth writes in *24/6, "When we go 24/7, we get to thinking that our well-being results from our own efforts. God gets taken out of the equation. We lose track of who made the universe. We begin thinking that the world can't run without us."[i]* The fact of the matter is, the world worked long before you were born and will continue to work long after you die.

Maybe you're thinking, with regards to your busyness and work, "I can stop anytime I want to." (you know, the classic addict phrase) Let's examine that claim. Does your phone sit next to your bed in case you need to answer something right away or so you don't miss a text? Do you bring it to the dinner table with you? Do your children have to call your name three or four times before you answer them because you're engrossed in your e-mail or Twitter feed? Does work regularly infringe upon family dinners and weekends? Did your kid just ask to borrow the car, and your first thought was, "Wait a minute, I thought she was nine years old"? If any of these scenarios ring true for you, then you may have a problem. You are not experiencing the freedom that God desires for your life. God wants us to be FREE!! He wants us to be free to be exactly who He created us to be and to do exactly what He created us to do.

Shifting from a life dictated by work and busyness to one characterized by intentional rest and Sabbath is not easy. It is completely countercultural and in many ways against our modus operandi. However, you may work out, and that's hard, but you do it because you recognize its benefits. Maybe you budget your money, and that's hard, but you do it because you recognize its benefits. Perhaps you are a parent, and that's hard just doing that, but you do it, and you strive to do it well (harder still) because you recognize its benefits. The benefit we gain from intentional rest and Sabbath is a balanced life; one lived out of obedience to His direction, one that will give you margin to rest, to hear what He has to say to you about your life, and one that is not enslaved to the need to create.

Try this thought experiment: What if I told you that you could have two months each year to simply rest? To read your Bible and to pray. To love and spend time with your family playing games or doing puzzles. To eat good food, but not spend time sweating over the stove. To sleep in and not answer phone calls or e-mails (to not even hear the phone ring or buzz at all). To laugh and to cry with good friends. To do the things that bring you life, not the things that are a part of your job description. To read a good book, but not one that will advance you at work. To drink a leisurely cup of coffee. To have a conversation with your spouse about your life, not your to-do list. To take a nap. To watch the sunset. To make love to your spouse. To look back on the past and reflect on how good God has been to you, and to look ahead with anticipation for what He will do. To lie down in green pastures and walk beside still waters instead of sitting in traffic. To say, "God, thank you that I am not what I do, but that I am simply your beloved child." If any of that sounds appealing to you, that is Sabbath. If you intentionally take a Sabbath once a week, you will experience this kind of rest and flourishing for close to two months every year. In this next year, may you experience two months of God's best for you.

[i] Sleeth, Matthew, et al.

Mike 'Fitz' Fitzpatrick is a follower of Jesus, husband, father of four kids, and the Family Ministry Pastor at Ginghamsburg Church in Tipp City, OH, in that order. You can connect with Fitz on Twitter at @mcfitzie.

Transformation Demands Fellowship

By Stephanie Bays

I remember being nine years young, and it was time to kiss my mom good night. It was our nightly routine. Yet, this night was different. As I approached my mom's bedroom doorway, she was on her knees praying. I waited for my mom to get up. I knew for sure she would arise. This was always our time. I stood there. She never got up. I walked away with my head hung low. Disappointment flooded my little soul.

I walked away thinking and saying to myself, "Who is this big guy that my mom won't even get up to kiss me goodnight?" I kept saying, "Who is this man?" Well, that moment left a big impression on my little spirit. My relationship with my mom was precious to me. I admired and adored my mom. I watched her clean the house and groom my siblings and me for school daily. She always made sure dinner was hot and ready for the family to gather at the table every evening. She was methodical. Her routine was solid. So, for my mom to break her routine of not kissing me good night, I was discombobulated! That was my time with my mom. My mom and I did this every night.

So, at the tender age of eleven, at a mid-week church service, the pastor asked if anyone wanted to give their life to Jesus. I humbly went to the altar to ask Jesus to come into my heart. I sobbed as I approached the altar. At that altar is where my life changed forever. I finally met the big guy my mom refused to budge from to fulfill our nightly routine. Now I see why my mom didn't interrupt her time with this big guy. This big guy's name was Jesus. From that moment to now, Jesus has been the center of my life. I started my journey into a relationship with Jesus.

Salvation brings us into this relationship with Jesus. John 3:3 states, Jesus said, *"I tell you the truth, no one can see the kingdom of God unless he is born again."* Romans 10:9 declares, *"That if you confess with thy mouth, "Jesus is Lord," and believe in your heart that God raised him from the dead, you will be saved."* It doesn't stop there. Remember the American Express commercial "membership has its privileges"? There are many believers who are living below their privileges. Privileges are benefits, rights bestowed upon us by God through Jesus. According to Psalm 68: 19, *"Blessed be the Lord, who daily loads us with benefits, even the God of our salvation."* Psalm 103:2 declares, *"Praise the Lord, O my soul, and forget not all his benefits."* (KJV).

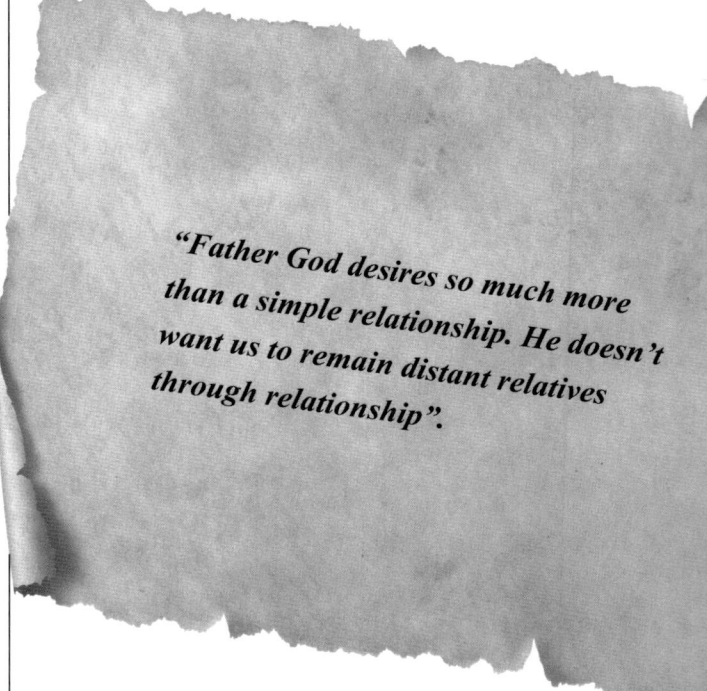

"Father God desires so much more than a simple relationship. He doesn't want us to remain distant relatives through relationship".

He wants us to go further than relationship. God desires fellowship with His children. The Bible is filled with stories about Jesus and small children. According to Matthew 19:14, Jesus said, *"Let the little children come to me, do not hinder them, for the kingdom of heaven belongs to such as these."* There is something that we as adults can learn from children. First, children are teachable. Second, children are quick to forgive. Third, children are all-trusting. 2 Corinthians 6:18 states that *"I will be a Father to you, and you will be my sons and daughters,"* says the Lord Almighty. Asking Jesus into your heart starts the Father-child relationship.

Relationship and fellowship are two different things. Relationship is two persons in the same ship, related because of DNA. Fellowship is two fellows related, in the same ship, who want to get to know each other. **You see, relationship doesn't constitute fellowship.** Father God desires for you to get to know Him. He doesn't want to remain a distant relative. Father God longs to have fellowship with you, just like I desired to have fellowship with my mom every night. Although my mom knew our relationship was important, her fellowship with this big guy, Jesus, trumped a goodnight kiss at that moment.

There are many ways we can experience fellowship with Our Father. King David declared in Psalm 139:7-10, *"Where can I go from your Spirit? Where can I flee from your presence? If I go up to the heavens, you are there; if I make my bed in the depths, you are there. If I rise on the wings of the dawn, if I settle on the far side of the sea; even there your hand will guide me, and your right hand will hold me fast. If I say, Surely the darkness will hide me; and the light become night around me, even the darkness will not be dark to you; the night will shine like the day, the darkness is as light to you."*

The Word of God is Necessary

King David is pleading, "God, You know everything about me. Therefore, I might as well get to know You!" If you want this fellowship with the Father, **The Word of God is necessary!** That's fellowship, People! The Word of God is a fundamental way for getting to know The Father. Both disciples Matthew and Mark denoted, *"Heaven and earth shall pass away, but my words shall not pass away."* There is a difference between being an informed believer versus being a transformed believer. An informed believer is one who is in relationship with Jesus, attends church faithfully, loves God, and even volunteers at church. However, this believer never really takes advantage of the benefits or privileges of the relationship. This believer allows the Bible to just sit on the mantle of the fireplace and collect dust.

This example reminds me of some familiar verses in James 1:22-25. *"Do not merely listen to the word, and so deceive yourselves. Do what it says. Anyone who listens to the word, and but does not do what it says is like a man who looks at his face in a mirror and, after looking at himself, goes away and immediately forgets what he looks like. But the man who looks intently into the perfect law of that gives freedom, and continues to do this, not forgetting what he has heard, but doing it-he will be blessed in what he does."* Romans 12:2 states, *"Do not conform any longer to the pattern of this world, but be transformed by the renewing of your mind. Then you will be able to test and approve what God's will is-his good, pleasing and perfect will.".* Lastly, Matthew 5:15 states, *"Neither do people light a lamp and put it under a bowl. Instead, they put it on its stand, and it gives light to everyone in the house.."*

As a believer, the more you fellowship with God, the more He will reveal Himself to you. The Word of God will no longer just be good information. This type of fellowship allows the Word to become revelation. Your present realities start to become spiritual realities. An exchange is beginning to emerge. The Word of God is no longer words on a page. The words start to speak to you, you hear

them, and adhere to the words. Father God desires for His people to become familiar with His Word. This fellowship becomes a conduit for transformation to take place.

Too often, as people of God, we don't see much change in our lives. Transformation doesn't take place by itself. **Transformation demands fellowship.** Fellowship is the share which one has in everything, such as partnership, communion, and intimacy. There's a partnership with intimacy that has developed because two have decided and committed to share everything. 2 Corinthians 6:14 declares, *"Do not be yoked together with unbelievers. For what do righteousness and wickedness have in common? Or what fellowship can light have with darkness?".* According to Philippians 3:10, *"I want to know Christ and the power of the fellowship of sharing in his sufferings, becoming like him in his death.".* Also, in 1 John 1:3, *"and our fellowship is with the Father and with his Son, Jesus Christ."*

Transformation is a thorough or dramatic change in form or appearance. Electrical power is the result of a conversion between two sources of energy, electricity and a natural source of energy, like oil. To generate the power, this process takes place at a power station. The movement within the turbines from the magnets with the copper coil causes the electrons (charged particles) to produce electricity. Likewise, when a person on purpose engages in fellowship with Jesus, power is released. According to Luke 8:43-46, *"And a woman was there who had been subject to bleeding for twelve years, but no one could heal her. She came up behind him and touched the edge of his cloak, and immediately her bleeding stopped. "Who touched me?"* Jesus asked. When they all denied it, Peter said, "Master, the people are crowding and pressing against you. But Jesus said, someone touched me; I know that power has gone out from me." Her pursuit, coupled with Jesus' presence, caused a conversion. A thorough and dramatic change in form and appearance took place. Her bleeding ceased immediately. **That's transformation, People of God!**

God's Call to "Come" is an Invitation to Fellowship

Moreover, prayer is a powerful tool to engage in fellowship with God. Prayer is simply communing with the Father. However, making prayer a lifestyle expedites transformation. I worked at Federal Express Corporation years ago as a Senior Customer Service representative. On some rare occasions, a customer might ask for their package to be expedited. Federal Express offered this speedy and prompt service. Unfortunately, this service was expensive due to an airline ticket being purchased in order for the package to arrive at its destination the same day.

It's through, what we may consider, the expensive lifestyle of prayer that causes permanent change to take place over time in a believer's life.

Jesus, on numerous occasions, left crowds of people to steal away and pray to the Father. He deemed prayer essential for daily fellowship. This fellowship afforded Jesus the ability to know the Father's will for His life. Moreover, John 5:19 says, *Jesus gave them this answer, "I tell you the truth, the Son can do nothing by himself; he can do only what he sees his Father doing, because whatever the Father does the Son also does."* A believer's life will never be the same once prayer becomes a priority. "The prayer of a righteous man is powerful and effective." expressed in James 5:16.

According to Mark 11:22-25, *"Have faith in God," Jesus answered. I tell you the truth, if anyone says to this mountain, "Go, throw yourself into the sea," and does not doubt in his heart but believes that what he says will happen, it will be done for him. Therefore, I tell you, whatever you ask in for prayer, believe that you have received it, and it will be yours."* Also, take into account the following verse in 3 John 1:2. *"Beloved I wish above all things that thou prosper and be in health even as thy soul propsereth.* (KJV) These verses are an indication that the Father enjoys seeing the fruits of His fellowship with His children. Let's not forget the account in James 1:17. *"Every good and perfect gift is from above, coming down from the Father of the heavenly lights, who does not change like shifting shadows."*

The invitation of come is seen again in Matthew 14:25-31. *During the fourth watch of the night Jesus went out to them, walking on the lake. When the disciples saw him walking on the lake, they were terrified. "It's a ghost," they said and cried out in fear. But Jesus immediately said to them: "Take courage! It is I. Don't be afraid." "Lord, if it's you," Peter replied, "tell me to* **come** *to you on the water."* **"Come,"** *he said."* Matthew 11:28-30 Jesus *declares, "come to me, all you who are weary and burdened, and I will give you rest. Take my yoke upon you and learn from me, for I am gentle and humble in heart, and you will find rest for your souls. For my yoke is easy and my burden is light."*. In James 4:8, **"Come** *near to God and he will* **come** *near to you."* These verses scream Father God's heart to engage in fellowship with his people, even in the midst of a storm!

I believe one of the most difficult truths to believe and discover is the spiritual reality that the God of the universe wants to hang out with flesh and bones. Why would a God, whom we can't see, desire to fellowship with human beings? Throughout the Bible, there are various accounts that attest to the truth of the Father's heart to fellowship with his sons and daughters. According to Joshua 10: 12-14, *"On the day the Lord gave the Amorites over to Israel, Joshua said to the Lord in the presence of Israel: "O sun, stand still over Gibeon, O moon, over the Valley of Aijalon." So, the sun stood still, and the moon stopped, till the nation avenged itself on its enemies, as it is written in the Book of Jashar. The sun stopped in the middle of the sky and delayed going down about a full day. There has never been a day like it before or since, a day when the Lord listened to a man. Surely the Lord was fighting for Israel."* God of the universe stopped the earth for one day for a man named Joshua. Truly, truly can you image what the only true God, your Heavenly Father, would do for you? **YOU, yes YOU!** We are His sons and daughters. *"How great is the love the Father has lavished on us, that we should be called children of God!"* according to 1 John 3:1. The Father longs to have fellowship with his people through Jesus.

Worship Has Its Role

King David is a great example of one who accepted God's call to **"come."** King David cherished his fellowship with God. His heart was after God. The Book of Psalms is filled with numerous songs and hymns illustrating King David's fellowship with God. By accepting His invitation to **"come,"** King David couldn't help but worship. Psalm 95: 6 declares, **"Come,** *let us bow down in worship. Let us kneel before the Lord our Maker."* **"Come,** *let us sing for joy to the Lord."* **Worship is our acceptance of the invitation from the Father.** Although King David didn't always do things right and in order, one thing he did get right and in order was his fellowship. He feared God. He knew God. King David not only adored God, but he was also in love with God. King David was unapologetically not ashamed to praise and worship God. One account is found in 2 Samuel 6:14. The verse states, *"David, wearing a linen ephod, danced before the Lord with all his might."* There were times King David allowed people, places, and pleasures to disrupt his godly decision-making.

However, one thing for sure that King David didn't allow was an interruption to his fellowship with God. Psalm 63:1-4 bears witness of this fact. *"O God, you are my God, earnestly I seek you; my soul thirsts for you, my body longs for you, in a dry and weary land where there is no water. I have seen you in the sanctuary and beheld your power and your glory. Because your love is better than life my lips will glorify you. I will praise you as long as I live, and in your name I will lift up my hands."* As long as there is seedtime and harvest, we will continue to eat the fruit from the tree of King David's fellowship with God. **Worship undoubtedly changes you.**

When fellowship has continuity, transformation is the result. King David's fellowship was earmarked by the glory of the Lord appearing throughout his life. When we hear the word "glory," one can't help but think of power and presence. Another way to see this is the term, weight. For instance, when Arnold Schwarzenegger was in his younger years, what would have been his glory? The answer would be his muscles. A genius' glory is his or her intelligence. The Bible has much to say about the "glory" and the glory of the Lord. Proverbs 16:31 implies, *"Gray hair is a crown of glory; it is obtained by following a righteous path.",* as well as *"The glory of young men is their strength,"* declares Proverbs 20:29. Likewise, as a son or daughter of God, what's your glory? God's nature is our glory! 2 Peter 1:3-4 declares, *"His divine power has given us everything we need for life and godliness through our knowledge of him who called us by his own glory and goodness. Through these he has given us his very great and precious promises, so that through them you may participate in the divine nature and escape the corruption in the world caused by evil desires.".* People of God, we have the same nature as Father God. Romans 8: 15-17 implies we are His children. *"For you did not receive a spirit that makes you a slave again to fear, but you have received the Spirit of sonship, and by him we cry, Abba, Father. The Spirit himself testifies with our spirit that we are God's children. Now if we are children, then we are heirs-heirs of God and co-heirs with Christ, if indeed we share in his sufferings in order that we may also share in his glory."*

People of God, in a marriage relationship, the husband and wife become one. Genesis 2:24 bears witness of this truth. *"For this reason a man will leave his father and his mother and be united to his wife, and they will become one flesh."* The oneness in the marriage will be earmarked through continued fellowship that they have with each other. Likewise, you can have the same fellowship with Father God like Jesus. According to John 15:4, *"Remain in Me, and I will remain in you. No branch can bear fruit by itself; it must remain in the vine."* The more you spend time with God, the more you become like Him. Oftentimes it has been said the longer a person is married to each other, the more they begin to look alike. Furthermore, the more a believer spends time with God's Word, the more God's thoughts will become their thoughts, and God's ways become their ways. Like King David proclaimed in Psalm 25:10, *"All of the ways of the Lord are loving and faithful.". 1 John 2:6 states, "Whoever claims to live in him must walk as Jesus did.".* Apostle Paul taught the Corinthian church, *"be imitators of me, just as I am in Christ."*

Beloved, when you accept the Father's call to **"come"** as the invitation to fellowship with Him, your worship will be earmarked by the glory of the Lord being lavished upon you by your Father. According to 2 Corinthians 3:18, *"But we all unveiled face, beholding as in a mirror the glory of the Lord, are being transformed into the same image from glory to glory, just as from the Lord, the Spirit."* You will experience oneness with God through fellowship. In John 17:22, Jesus said, *"The glory which You have given Me I have given to them, that they may be one, just as We are one.".* Father God is waiting for you. Get in the ship. Don't remain a distant relative. **COME.**

Stephanie Y. Bays is a welcome speaker for not-for-profit organizations, businesses, and universities. She enjoys spending time with family and resides in Maumee.

A Prophetic Word for 2022

Mark 15:15 *"And he said to them, "Go into all the world and preach the Gospel to all creation."*

Acts 1:8 *"...but you will receive power when the Holy Spirit has come upon you; and you shall be My witnesses both in Jerusalem, and in all Judea and Samaria and even to the remotest part of the earth."*

I believe the Lord is saying this to us in this season;

My commands have not changed since My Word was written by My Spirit. I am still calling you to go into the entire world and preach the Gospel. However, look at what I am doing in this season. This nation is the most prosperous and powerful nation to exist on the face of the earth. For a time now, I have been bringing the nations to you. I have brought the people from South America to you, the people of China to you, the people from the Mid-East to you, and most recently, the people of Haiti to you. For what purpose, you ask? You think they will overrun your systems, but I have brought them to share in the Gospel, which I have called you to preach to the nations.

Covid closed the world, but I stirred up the world to bring them to you. This is nothing new. When I gave Solomon wisdom, discernment, and knowledge, what happened? Men came from all the peoples to hear the wisdom of Solomon, from all the kings of the earth who had heard of his wisdom. (1 Kings 4:34) See what I have done. Do you see? I have brought and continue to bring the nations to you to preach the Gospel. Church, do not be afraid of these people. Go and embrace them with My love. It is time and is always the time for the Church to rise up and welcome those into your community, make them disciples.

Jim Pinkelman

To Live by One's Own Faith

By Denise Emerine

"Behold, his soul which is lifted up is not upright in him: ***but the just shall live by his faith"*** (Habakkuk 2:4, my emphasis). The phrase I emphasize here is familiar to Christians all over the world. For centuries "living by faith" has motivated the daily decisions of believers in every generation.

Habakkuk's prophecy here is the first mention of living by faith. Later, in the New Testament, the Apostle Paul invokes the phrase three times. Today, Habakkuk 2:4 remains one of the most preached texts of all Scripture. It has formed the basis of many church doctrines. To "live by faith" speaks of how we are justified and sanctified, how we find peace and joy, how we obtain victory over sin. These are all wonderful applications of Habakkuk's powerful truth.

Yet, I want to focus on the historical context of this passage. When Habakkuk spoke of "living by faith," it was to help Israel know how to face a coming crisis. Here was an eternal truth meant to help the people navigate a calamity that was about to befall them. Also, it was delivered during a time very similar to our present day.

Habakkuk had received a dreadful burden from the Lord about a destructive calamity coming upon Israel. At the time, God's laws were being despised and ignored. Judges ruled in favor of the wicked. The wealthy used God's law to rob the poor and build up fortunes through fraudulent practices. Covetousness became a public obsession.

Habakkuk was grieved deeply by everything God showed him. Scripture calls this *"the burden which Habakkuk the prophet did see"* (1:1). Worldliness had infiltrated the church. Morality had collapsed in the surrounding nations. As Habakkuk beheld all this, he cried, *"Lord, why all this iniquity? Why do the wicked triumph over the righteous?"*

"Why do You show me iniquity and cause me to see trouble? For plundering and violence are before me. There is strife and contention arises. Therefore the law is powerless, and justice never goes forth. For the wicked surround the righteous, therefore perverse judgment proceeds." (1:3-4).

Just when the prophet became overwhelmed by his burden, God gave him a vision.

"Look among the nations and watch – Be utterly astounded! For I will work a work in your days which you would not believe, though it be told to you." (1:5). The Lord told Habakkuk, *"I'm going to raise up a rod of correction to bring judgment on the land. And it will be My doing. If I told you how swiftly it will come and how terrible it will be, you would not believe it."*

Here is the word Habakkuk received about God's rod of correction: *"The Chaldeans are coming! They're going to march through the breadth of the earth devouring all in their path."* (1:6).

This terrible vision shook Habakkuk in his core. He tells us, *"When I heard, my belly trembled; my lips quivered at the voice; rottenness entered into my bones, and I trembled in myself, that I might rest in the day of trouble: when he comes upon the people, he will invade them with his troops."* (3:16)

Now Habakkuk reflected on his calling as a prophet. He knew the godly remnant in Israel would come to him asking, "How can we get through these terrible things to come? If our nation and those around us are under God's humbling, what will we do? How will we live? What does the Lord require of us?"

I hear the same questions being asked by God's people right now as our world faces increasing disaster. The upheaval we're seeing is most certainly the work of God. Once again, He has risen up to deal with covetousness and Sodom-like perversity. He also has raised His rod against the greedy robbing of widows and defrauding of the poor.

How did Habakkuk respond? He hid himself away with the Lord in prayer. He set his heart to wait on God for a word to His people. Here is how the prophet began his prayer: *"I will stand on my guard post, and station myself on the rampart: I will keep watch to see what He will speak to me, how I may reply* ***when I am corrected.*** *" (2:1, my emphasis).* Notice Habakkuk began by opening his heart to correction. He prayed, *"Lord, let Your work begin by first examining me."*

We know Habakkuk had already questioned God's slowness to answer his prayers. *"How long shall I cry, and You will not hear?"* (1:2). I wonder if Habakkuk had to deal with a bit of "Jonah syndrome" in himself. He knew he dare not gloat, saying, "I told you so," as God brought down the proud.

The Lord did give Habakkuk a word, and it changed the prophet's prayer from, "Why have You withheld judgment?" to, "Lord, as You judge, remember Your mercy." *"I have heard Your speech, and was afraid: O'Lord, revive Your work in the midst of the years…in wrath remember mercy"* (3:2).

Habakkuk was instructed to write down the vision.

The incredible word Habakkuk received was meant not only for his day but for every generation, down to our present time. *"At the end it shall speak"* (2:3). God made it clear to Habakkuk this word wasn't for the proud or those who turn to flesh trusting in the promises of men.

Right now, many in God's house are placing their hope in government bailouts – trillions intended to save the economy, rescue the financial system, provide millions of jobs. They're hoping the brightest leaders in our land will solve our problems and get us back to prosperity. Oh, how arrogant to think money can correct man's ways! How proud to believe our currency can withstand God's righteous ways.

"By faith" is the only way God's people are ever able to face a disaster or affliction. It was the only way in Habakkuk's day; it was the only way in the Old Testament generation. Also, it was the only way in New Testament times. Now in our present calamity, the same foundational truth stands. "The just shall live by his faith."

Yet what does this mean, to live by one's faith? God's Word shows us it means more than simply believing. To live by one's faith *is to see God's hand and His holiness in all calamities and shaking. The Lord is known by the judgment He executes."* (Psalm 9:16).

"When Your hand is lifted up, (the wicked) will not see" (Isaiah 26:11). The world doesn't see God lifting His hand to bring humbling. However, those who live by faith readily acknowledge that what we are seeing is God's hand at work. This is His holiness being established. He is keeping His Word.

If we are to live by faith, we must have a reverential fear of God's power. It is impossible not to see His awesome might at work in the world today. Think of it: *Scripture says, "The rich man's wealth is his strong city."* (Proverbs 18:11). Yet in just two weeks' time, God shook the earth by shutting down its mighty businesses and the world's provision for a year.

What else but the power of God could cause men to lose confidence in their amassed fortunes by causing trillions to dissolve in a matter of weeks? His judgment is clearly at work. Yet, it is His mercy which He always shows by exposing the fraud and corruption taking place in worldwide financial institutions. It is His righteousness which He establishes by cutting off the deceptions of mortgage companies who defrauded the poor and left them homeless.

We know God does not delight in humbling. Scripture says it gives Him no pleasure. Yet His Word says all gold and silver will be devoured by moles (Isaiah 2:20). It will happen *"for fear of the Lord, and for the glory of His majesty, when He rises to shake terribly the earth"* (2:19). It is all meant to bring the awesome fear of God to all nations.

These two sides of God's nature – righteous judgment and merciful love – require we live by faith.

The same God who wields His mighty power to "shake all things terribly" is the same loving Father who acts as our shield and keeper. Consider: on the one hand, Isaiah tells us, *"(Sinners) declare their sin as Sodom, they hide it not. Woe unto their soul! For they have brought evil upon themselves."* (Is.3:9). Yet the very next verse tells us, *"Say to the righteous, that it shall be well with them: they shall eat the fruit of their doings."* (Is. 3:10). Despite all the terrible shaking, those who live by faith will be kept safe and well.

Right now, I believe the Church needs a refresher course on God's majesty and power, such as Job was given. The Lord said to Job, in essence, "What is all this dark, hopeless talk I hear from you? Stand up and listen to Me: "I laid the foundation of the earth. I made the light and the darkness. I created the rain, snow, ice, and wind. I gave wings to the birds of the air. I feed the beasts of the field, and I control all of nature. Tell Me, Job, who can thunder with a voice like Mine? Who can look into every man's heart and see its condition? Who is able to identify the arrogant, locate them and bring them low?

Beloved, the same God who knows the name and address of every proud person also knows your name, your address, your condition. He will keep you in His heart all of your days through every calamity. To accept this is to live by faith.

"If I live by faith, I will not fear for the future of God's church in disastrous times."

"Upon this rock I will build My Church; and the gates of hell shall not prevail against it" Matthew 16:18). This pledge from Jesus has emboldened the faith of generations. It is meant to sustain us now in our present global crisis.

We also have this warning, *"In the latter times some shall depart from faith."* (1 Timothy 4:1). In perilous times such as ours, leaders will arise *"having a form of godliness, but denying the power thereof."* (2 Timothy 3:5). Under the influence of these false leaders, the love of many believers will grow cold or lukewarm. Others will lose their faith altogether and fall away from Christ.

Yet, according to Joel, at the very same time God is going to pour out His Spirit on all flesh (Joel 2:28-29). The psalmist writes, *"You send forth Your spirit, they are created; and You renew the face of the earth"* (Psalm 104:30). God's Spirit has never been depleted. He can pour out as He pleases. Whenever this happens, *"Ten men shall take hold...of the skirt of him that is (a believer), saying, we will go with you: for we have heard that God is with you."* (Zechariah 8:23).

Are you getting the picture? In the midst of catastrophic times, there will be a great harvest. The unsaved are going to turn to believers crying, "God is clearly with you. Tell me, how can I know this peace?"

If I am to live by my faith, I must do as Noah did and build an ark to ride out the storm.

"By faith Noah...moved with fear, prepared an ark to the saving of his house" (Hebrews 11:7). The ark that Noah built represents Jesus Christ. There is no other safe place on earth. When Isaiah prophesied of a king coming to reign in righteousness, he was clearly describing Christ. *"A man shall be as a hiding place from the wind, and a cover from the tempest; as rivers of water in a dry place, as the shadow of a great rock in a weary land"* (Isaiah 32:2).

All over the world, people are desperately searching for a safe place to hide their money. Multitudes are buying guns to protect their families for what they believe will be a dark time of "every man for himself." These include Bible-believing Christians.

Yet, there is no place of guaranteed safety on earth except to abide in Jesus. I don't state this as some empty theology that Christians often say thoughtlessly. For over 2000 years, those who have trusted in Jesus for safety have proven God's Word faithful, *"The name of the Lord is a strong tower: the righteous run to it, and is safe"* (Proverbs 18:10).

We also know that through the centuries, those who have

trusted in Jesus have suffered much. Since the time of the cross, they have been martyred, some viciously. New Testament believers lost their homes and lands and lived in caves. Since that time, multitudes have lost jobs, homes, family members in times of calamity. Many others have died in wars and from natural disasters.

Beloved, no true preacher of God's Word will ever promise that you won't suffer, that you won't lose property, that your lifestyle will be protected. There is a great cloud of witnesses in heaven who say to all of us who love Jesus, "It is true that in Christ we were safe – *eternally safe.* His grace was sufficient for every crisis. Yes, there were seasons of pain, suffering, and hard times, but no trial can ever take you out of Christ, the *Ark of safety."*

It doesn't matter how downcast you get, God will never forsake you! Satan's great work against God's people is discouragement. Within moments of enjoying a spiritual victory, every believer becomes a target for the powers of hell. The devil attacks us with his lies about our marriage, our friendships, our calling, and the list goes on. He replays in our minds every sin, failure, and foolish thing we've ever done. By the time he's finished, we're crying, "Lord, I'll never make it unless You come."

David was brought so low by a demonic spirit that he was dumbfounded in God's presence. *"I as a deaf man, heard not; and I was a dumb man that opened not my mouth. So, I was as a man...in whose mouth is no accusations"* (Ps. 38:13-14). This last phrase means "a man who has no arguments left." David was saying, "Lord, I'm too discouraged to even lift my hand. I can't pray because I'm too confused to speak. My spirit is drained and empty. I have nothing to say."

I tell you, David's trial was not unique. I have read many biographies of devout men and women whom the Lord used mightily, and every one of these people struggled through the same kind of crippling discouragement. David voiced the universal cry of the righteous soul that endures an attack of discouragement. *"I am ready to halt (fall), and my sorrow is continually before me"* (Ps. 38:17). David was saying, "Lord, I'm not going to make it. I'm at my absolute end, about to fall."

If you're enduring an attack from a demonic spirit of discouragement, I propose you do these three things: (1) Do not try to maneuver your way out of your trial. The battle is far beyond your human skill or power to wage. (2) When the attack comes, don't think it is unusual. God allows this kind of testing with His saints. (3) Go to prayer, giving the Holy Spirit time to do His work. When you're under discouragement, you won't feel like praying. But you still must go to your secret place to be in Jesus' presence. It is the Spirit's job to lift you out of your pit.

In such low times, the Lord is very patient with us. He knows our condition, and He sympathizes with us. If you don't have the strength to speak, reach out to Him in your spirit, and trust the Spirit to do His work. Say in your heart, "Lord, I know Your Spirit abides in me. I know You have been sent to comfort me, strengthen me, and reveal the mind of Christ to me. Holy Spirit, I turn to You now in simple <u>faith.</u> Speak to my heart Your words of comfort. I have no strength left; You have to lift me up and lead me."

Dare to believe He will speak to you. You're not going to faint. Indeed, you'll come out of your trial more victorious because your <u>faith</u> will have been tested and tried as gold. Watch and see the Lord fulfill every promise He has ever made to you.

I leave you with this wonderful promise from 1 Peter: 3-9: *"According to His abundant mercy He has begotten us again to a living hope through the resurrection of Jesus Christ from the dead, to an inheritance incorruptible and undefiled and that does not fade away, reserved in heaven for you, who are kept by the power of God through <u>faith</u> for salvation ready to be revealed in the last time. In this you greatly rejoice, though now for a little while, if need be, you are in heaviness by various trials, that the genuineness of your <u>faith,</u> being much more precious than gold that perishes, though it is tested by fire, may be found to praise, honor, and glory at the revelation of Jesus Christ, whom having not seen you love. Though now you do not see Him, yet believing, you rejoice with joy inexpressible and full of glory, receiving the end of your <u>faith</u>--the salvation of your souls."*

May He find you faithful to Him until the end of your days.

Denise currently serves as the Director of the Greater Toledo House of Prayer. She also works alongside business owners in the nation to build prayer rooms in their companies. She is partnered with ministries in Israel to build bridges of relationship between the two countries. Denise is married and has ten beautiful grandchildren.

Dreams of Euclidean Lines

By Todd Hostetler

Over the years I have come to experience insight from the Holy Spirit in a number of ways. I have realized that there is wisdom in not limiting my expectations of how He will speak and reveal Himself to me. For the purposes of this article, I want to explain one of the ways He personally reveals things to me. I have come to notice when I am sleeping that there are different phases and levels of sleep. For me, one of the most dynamic periods is just before I awake. It is that phase when you are still asleep but getting ready to awaken. The best way that I can describe it is as twilight because twilight is that brief moment between day and night or a similar period of time between night and day. When I am sleeping, twilight is that precious moment of receptivity between sleeping and waking. That is a moment that I find the Holy Spirit often speaks to me.

The twilight we experience when we are awake is one of the purest times of the day. Be it at dusk or dawn, the sun is beyond the horizon and unseen, but the rays of light refract through the atmosphere and create that peaceful and marvelous palate of colors in the sky. Photographers will tell you that the best light for photographs comes in the pure soft light of twilight or what they refer to as the golden hour in the morning or the blue hour in the evening. That light is the most clarified, undefiled, and unpolluted light. Therefore, it results in the most filtered and concentrated colors. Because the light has no hard contrasts, it tends not to have hard shadows.

That is what I feel like in that moment of sleep that I refer to as twilight because I am getting ready to awaken, but I am in an open and receiving mode, and that which comes is so soft and pure, with extreme clarity and powerful imagery. There are no shadows of confusion or doubt, just the untainted light of Jesus and His revelation. When I am in that twilight of sleep, I have often had clear dreams, images, insights, or sometimes I have just heard things or felt things from the spirit realm. I treasure those moments, and they have encouraged, strengthened, challenged, and taught me.

A few years ago, my wife and I were out of town for an event in the midst of a busy week. In the middle of that week, in the hotel room, I had this "twilight" revelation experience shortly before I woke up. It was brief and simple, but I heard a phrase in my sleep as clear as if the voice were right by my side of the bed. Then I heard the same phrase again, just as clearly in my sleep. Then, I immediately woke up from a state of sleep, and the words that I heard were still clear in my mind. A dramatic experience, right? So you would expect the words that I heard would be dramatic. You would expect there to be an "aha" moment as my mind became fully awake. However, there was no mistaking what I had heard, but it did not bring an "aha" moment with it. The phrase I heard was two words. Two words that meant nothing to me on that morning. The two words were "Euclidean lines."

I have a love for learning that can, at times, be unsatiable. I love history and science. I also have a growing interest and passion for the creativity of art. I revel in studying those disciplines and discovering the Biblical truths that are born out of each of those subjects when examined through the lens of the Bible and a Biblical perspective. However, I have absolutely no interest in one area of study at all: mathematics!

Mathematics was always a challenge at school, and I have taken great joy throughout the years following my college experience to snub my nose at anything to do with math. It felt so good knowing as an adult, I could choose to learn about whatever I wanted, and nobody could force me to do anything with any of the branches of mathematics. So for three decades, I successfully navigated my way around math equations or theories.

Now, of course, having spurned math entirely for decades. I was unaware on that morning of my twilight that Euclid had anything to do with math. I had no idea that Euclidean lines had any reference to math at all. When I awoke after having heard the phrase "Euclidean lines," I knew that Euclid was someone in history. That was fine. As I already established, I love history. However, I thought that Euclid was a Greek philosopher much like Socrates, Aristotle, or Plato. Operating under that assumption, I had no idea what Euclidean lines could be or if that meant anything historically. So I asked my wife immediately, "Is there such a thing as Euclidean lines?" She said she thought there was but was not certain, and she definitely did not know what they might be.

I quickly searched the Web and found there is indeed something called Euclidean lines. My curiosity was peaked. Even though I had learned that Euclid was not a Greek philosopher but rather a Greek mathematician, I was still compelled to learn more. Why had the Spirit of God spoken to me at twilight and said, "Euclidean lines"?

I will save you the time of googling it for those like me who did not know about Euclid. Euclid lived in the 4th-century bc and is best known for his "The Elements" treatise on geometry. No passing fancy, it was a substantial effort as there were 13 volumes to Euclid's "The Elements." In years past, I would have felt like I had wasted my time discussing such things as an ancient Greek text about geometry. But having heard those two words "Euclidean lines" spoken in the twilight of sleep that morning, I am now surprisingly delighted to share with you some principles from Euclidean geometry that actually reveal some spiritual truths. For when the Holy Spirit speaks to you about Euclidean lines, you will passionately pursue the spiritual truths He is leading you to. In fact, there is so much that I have learned and so much more yet to discover that I can only touch on some highlights that excited me in this article.

Definitions and Axiom's

In his book, "The Elements," Euclid begins by laying out some basic definitions for geometry. One of those definitions is about lines, thus the phrase, "Euclidean lines"! Then upon these definitions, Euclid builds some axioms or self-evident truths. Finally, using these definitions and axioms, Euclid then postulates his theories which are still taught and respected today over 2,000 years later. Since this whole adventure began with Euclidean lines, what exactly does Euclid say about lines; what are his definitions? To begin with, he defines a line as "length without breadth." While that may not be how we would describe a line if asked to do so, it does make sense that a line does not have depth. It is a one-dimensional figure. Then he adds this to the definition: "The extremities of lines are points." We can easily visualize this regardless of how long or short a line is. If it has an ending, that ending is a single point. Euclid goes on to say that a straight line is a line that lies evenly with the points on itself". That is just a way of saying that a line is nothing more than a straight progression of points, all laid out in a row and touching each other with no space between them. So far, this is all easy enough that even I can comprehend and visualize what he is describing.

Then Euclid goes a step further and talks about lines that make up a surface or a plane. In the same way that points aligned next to each other in a row make a line, lines aligned next to each other in a row with no space between them will create a flat surface or a plane. Hurrah! I am still with him. Euclid hasn't lost me yet.

All of this is one or two-dimensional, so it is relatively easy to picture and understand. However, what is the spiritual truth that we are to learn from this? That is what I was having a hard time perceiving. Then I realized that

"The Bible does talk to us about points, lines, and planes, so I could simply let the Bible describe to me what spiritual truths were to be revealed in points, lines, and planes."

Points

In the New King James Bible, the word "points" surprisingly appears only five times in the entire Bible. We see one of the places in Numbers 33, as the Israelites are getting close to entering the Promised Land. As Moses prepares to recap the history of their travels from Egypt to their present position, he begins by saying this:

"These are the journeys of the children of Israel, who went out of the land of Egypt by their armies under the hand of Moses and Aaron. 2 Now Moses wrote down the starting points of their journeys at the command of the Lord. And these are their journeys according to their starting points:" Numbers 33:1-2 NKJV

Then Moses chronicles, point by point, every place they went, and every place they camped. It's a running list of "they departed" here and "they camped" there. Point by point, Moses makes a line of their journey to the Promised Land.

The word "points' is only mentioned twice in the New Testament. One of those occasions is in Hebrews chapter 4. The author of Hebrews is talking about the Israelites who failed to enter the Promised Land because of their disobedience and disbelief. Although they did not enter the promised "rest" of the Promised Land, there remains a promise of His rest today! We are encouraged to be diligent to enter that promised rest.

Towards the end of that chapter, we read of the great High Priest we have in Jesus, who has prepared the way for us to enter into His rest. Finally, we find the word points in verse 15, where we learn Jesus was in all points tempted just as we are, yet without sin.

"For we do not have a High Priest who cannot sympathize with our weaknesses, but was in all points tempted as we are, yet without sin." Hebrews 4:15 NKJV

There is nothing you have faced, no failure in your life that Jesus was not tempted with Himself. Point by point,

He overcame and did not sin so that if we would believe on Him we will find that promised rest in His salvation. Just as Moses gave a point-by-point line from Egypt to the Promised Land, we now understand that Jesus has gone before us point by point to lay out a line of salvation in Him. Remember that, as we will come back to that in a few moments.

As in Euclid's definitions, we see how points all align together to create a line in the Bible. It is a line to His promised rest for those who accept the sacrificial work of Jesus on their behalf.

Lines

This understanding of points brings us to the beginning of our understanding of lines. Let's again let the Bible explain things for us as we see what it reveals to us about lines, which are made up of points one after another. All those points together make a line, and this is a spiritual picture of movement forward, an advance. This is the Christian life lived in Jesus. With our eyes on Jesus, we will advance point by point in a straight line that progresses into His promises. That point-by-point progression of a line represents our growth from faith to faith and from victory to victory in Him.

As we spend time with Jesus and in the Word, we are led, taught, and directed forward in a line of revelation. The prophet Isaiah referred to this when he spoke about building on our knowledge of the Bible line by line.

"But the word of the Lord was to them, "Precept upon precept, precept upon precept, Line upon line, line upon line, Here a little, there a little," That they might go and fall backward, and be broken And snared and caught." Isaiah 28:13 NKJV

Because they didn't learn with lesson upon lesson, line by line, they did not advance, but instead, they fell backward and were snared by life. If you believe that the Word is the revelation of Jesus to you, you will gain understanding line by line in the Word. With each line of understanding comes a new depth of revelation. Each revelation builds upon the ones already learned, and your growth becomes exponential. It is not just in the knowledge that we grow line by line. It is faith by faith as we learn how to apply His Word daily. Recall what Paul told us in Romans:

[16]"For I am not ashamed of the gospel of Christ, for it is the power of God to salvation for everyone who believes, for the Jew first and also for the Greek. [17]For in it the righteousness of God is revealed from faith to faith; as it is written, "The just shall live by faith." Romans 1:16-17 NKJV

We are not ashamed of the gospel of Jesus but rather passionate and unable to stop talking about Jesus because it just pours out of us. This is an intriguing thought. Realize that the idea of not being ashamed of the gospel works both ways. We are never to be ashamed of the gospel, and as we will live boldly in His truth, we will find we will also never be put to shame for our belief in Him. In other words, as I stand on the promises of Jesus, I will never be left ashamed because His Word did not work! If I stand and continue to stand, I will see the evidence of His promises made manifest in this life for all to see.

The gospel is the righteousness of God, the purity and rightness of God. That righteousness makes all things right in Him. Applying the gospel line by line results in corrupted things being made aright in Jesus. Then Paul says this righteousness is revealed from faith to faith. That indicates that it all begins with the faith of Jesus that He imparted to each who believes in Him. You received His faith within you when you believed, so you have all the faith you require to advance in that line of progression to His destinations for you. Also, as you grow from exercising your faith and witness His victories in your life, your faith will increase all the more. Your faith will grow step by step or line by line as you believe His Word, live it out and see it come to pass in your life.

The Measuring Line

There is another interesting use of the word "line" in the Bible. Twice we see God speak of the line He used to lay out the foundations of the world. He refers to a standard of measurement or a measuring line like that used in construction work. We see this example when God speaks to Job about His creative work in this natural world.

[4]"Where were you when I laid the foundations of the earth? Tell Me, if you have understanding. [5]Who determined its measurements? Surely you know! Or who stretched the line upon it? [6]To what were its foundations fastened? Or who laid its cornerstone, [7]When the morning stars sang together, And all the sons of God shouted for joy? Job 38:4-7 NKJV

God stretched out His measuring line and laid the foundations of the earth. Notice that in the same verses where God speaks of this measuring line, He also points out to us that the morning stars were singing together. The reason that is interesting is that when God once again speaks of His creative work to David, He speaks of not just the creation of the earth but of the skies above, the endless cosmos. Notice that once more, He references the measuring line and the stars.

"The heavens declare the glory of God; And the firmament shows His handiwork. [2]Day unto day utters speech, And

night unto night reveals knowledge. ³There is no speech nor language Where their voice is not heard. ⁴Their line has gone out through all the earth, And their words to the end of the world. In them He has set a tabernacle for the sun," Psalm 19:1-4 NKJV

Like all of His creation, the stars speak and reveal His glory every moment, night and day. In verse 4, the word we read as "line" comes from a Hebrew word that means "their voice"! Lines are a progression from point to point to a destination. Now we see that creation itself, all of creation, speaks of the glory of God and reveals His righteousness and power. All of creation is tied in a direct line to its creator. You can say that God Himself speaks through all creation. He speaks His truth and righteousness through all creation directly from the spirit realm to the natural realm. Are we taking the time to listen and hear?

"For ever since the creation of the world His invisible nature and attributes, that is, His eternal power and divinity, have been made intelligible and clearly discernible in and through the things that have been made (His handiworks). So [men] are without excuse [altogether without any defense or justification]," Romans 1:20 Amplified Bible

He is speaking His glory in a line from the spirit realm to the natural realm so that we can hear. Everything in nature speaks and calls us to see Him and to seek to know Him more. Remember, God referred to the speaking of the stars (or creation) as a line. Euclidean lines can be endless. His measuring line used to create all things is a line that speaks from heaven to earth. Lines reveal to us the power and importance of speaking. God spoke all things into existence. It was His measuring line of creation. There is power in the words that we speak as well. As we seek Him in the Word, we will grow and learn verse by verse or with line-by-line revelation. This develops our faith so that we can speak words that align (or line up) with His Word and His promises. Our words should be in line with His Word instead of being in line with the carnal world that is opposed to God's things.

God's measuring line was His line of speech that laid out and established the earth's foundations. Our measuring line needs to be the Words of faith we speak! If our measuring line is speaking in agreement with His Words, there is no limit to what He can do through us. His victories will be beyond our ability to measure in this life. Are your words in a proper line with His line of speech, with what He has already spoken?

The Surveyor's Line

This imagery of measuring line is that of a surveyor's tool called a surveyor's line. The prophet Jeremiah speaks to us

about this very thing.

So, we have seen multiple references to the measuring line of God, and the imagery is that of a surveyor's line. This is a line that a surveyor uses to measure the distance between one place and another. The prophet Jeremiah speaks to us about this very thing.

³⁸"Behold, the days are coming, says the Lord, that the city shall be built for the Lord from the Tower of Hananel to the Corner Gate. ³⁹The surveyor's line shall again extend straight forward over the hill Gareb; then it shall turn toward Goath." Jeremiah 31:38-39 NKJV

Prophesy spoke a truth to those who heard it when it was spoken, but it also has a truth for the present church age we live in and a truth for the end times. In the church age we live in today, we are cities built for the Lord. In Matthew's Gospel, Jesus refers to us as cities on a hill whose light cannot be hid. Now Jeremiah describes a line that extends all the way to the hill of Gareb and on to Goath. This is a line that ties the city directly to Goath. It is the surveyor's line! Jesus is our constant source of strength and power, and that strength and power are illustrated to us in the surveyor's line. What is the significance of Goath? Goath is another name for…Golgotha! That's right, the place of the cross, the cross on the hill of Golgotha where the price for sin was paid in full.

God speaks of the surveyor's line as a direct, unbending, unaltering line between Calvary and our lives in Jesus. His strength, power, and victory come in an uninterrupted straight line to you and me if we believe and are willing to grow in Him and mature spiritually with line-by-line revelation that develops our faith.

Planes

The next step in Euclidean geometry is the understanding of "planes." We have already established the importance of points. Points all align in a progression that creates a line. Also, we established the importance of the "line" Biblically. The next thing to envision is what happens when you lay a line next to a line, and another line next to that, and so forth. Just as one point after another will make a line, one line after another makes a plane. According to Euclid, a plane is defined this way, "parallel straight lines are straight lines which, being in the same plane and being produced indefinitely in both directions, do not meet one another in either direction."

That sounds like a lot, but we can easily visualize this as an infinite number of lines that all point to Jesus and His promised rest in the truth of His Word. Every day as I gather a fresh revelation from the Word as I build my faith and as I walk in His strength and victory, I advance toward that rest. The beauty of His Word and truth is that it is not just one-dimensional. I get revelation line by line, and as I. continue to add line to line, I get a second dimension. Each line goes forward toward Jesus, one dimension. But as I add lines one next to the other, I also get expansive movement or width instead of just linear movement or length.

As I learn more from His Word line by line (linear), I also grow spiritually, and this expansion in me adds another dimension (width) in me. Just as Euclid's lines expand into a second dimension, we can visualize and he describers as a plane. Can you picture this plane in your mind? It is flat but has both length and width.

Plane is a geometric term that gives us a picture of a flat surface over a broad expanse. There is also a similar word that is used in geography that also describes an expansive flat surface. That word is plain. The Bible speaks of this flat-surfaced broad expanse many times. It is a reference to flat terrains. One of the places we see this term used is in the book of Zechariah.

"'Who are you, O great mountain? Before Zerubbabel you shall become a plain! And he shall bring forth the capstone With shouts of "Grace, grace to it!"'" Zechariah 4:7 NKJV

As we advance through life point by point and line by line in His direction, we will eventually come upon a mountain in our path. Mountains are difficult to traverse and can be overwhelming. Seeing a mountain in our path can cause us to pause in our advance toward His rest. They can psychologically defeat us, leading us to cease our forward movement before traversing the mountain. Satan puts mountains before us for just this cause. Zechariah speaks to us about the moment mountains in our path confront us. Jesus is the "capstone" spoken of, and when we bring the Word of God to any situation, we can speak to the mountain in His authority and power. Regardless of what the mountain is, it will become flat and level before us, easy to traverse.

Planes in geometry are a second dimension, a different dimension than points and lines. As we grow in Jesus and His Word line by line, we will experience a different dimension as well. We will bring the spiritual dimension to this natural dimension, and the things of the spirit realm always supersede the things of the natural realm. The more lines we add (length), the more expansive our plane becomes (width). That spiritual plane always makes the mountains of this life easy to traverse.

Parallel Lines

Let's go back for a moment to the definition we looked at for planes. "parallel straight lines are straight lines which, being in the same plane and being produced indefinitely in both directions, do not meet one another in either direction." Simply stated, two parallel lines never meet. That seems to me like the next step in our understanding of how Euclidean lines reveal spiritual truths to us. When you look up the word "parallel" in the Bible, you find that it is only mentioned one time in the New King James and not at all in many other translations. That makes the single reference to it pretty interesting in my mind. It is found in the book of Ezekiel.

"And a wall which was outside ran parallel to the chambers, at the front of the chambers, toward the outer court; its length was fifty cubits." Ezekiel 42:7 NKJV

Yeah, I know, not overly impressive at first glance. But then, when we consider two things, it really speaks a final truth to us about the beauty of Euclidean lines as they reveal spiritual truths to us. In that verse, we again see that measurements of the future temple are being taken that Ezekiel sees prophetically. In this verse, the wall described as parallel is making reference to a hedge, a hedge that runs along the outside wall of the chambers of the temple. According to Gill's Exposition of the Entire Bible: *"This wall separated and distinguished the chambers from the outward court, as well as was a protection of them; and signifies the grace and power of God, which separates his true churches from the world, and is the security of them;."*

So we are getting a picture of a wall or hedge that runs parallel to the temple of God to shield it and protect it. It is a picture of the power of the Holy Spirit running parallel to you in this life as you run your race in a linear fashion and grow in your spiritual maturity heading toward His promised rest in Him in this life.

I also found that this Hebrew word we read as "parallel" is used earlier in the book of Ezekiel. The Hebrew word is "ummah," and the verse below translates it as "against."

"Behold, I have made your face strong against their faces, and your forehead strong against their foreheads." Ezekiel 3:8 NKJV

God is telling Ezekiel that the people will not hear the word God has given him to speak. They are hard-hearted and will not listen. However, God says that He will make the face and forehead of the prophet strong against theirs. As you bump heads with the world, you can be at peace because the Holy Spirit is in us and is like that parallel hedge that moves alongside us. When you are face to face with those who oppose Jesus in you, keep speaking the Word and moving forward in faith. The Holy Spirit is with you, paralleling you and acting as that hedge between you and the adversary. He parallels you so when the world faces you with opposition, you can look them in the eye with the boldness of the Holy Spirit, and they will be the ones who flinch.

Conclusion

I believe that when the Holy Spirit spoke to me in that dream and simply said, "Euclidean lines," He wanted me to see there is a difference between how the things in this natural world work as compared to the things of the spiritual realm. We tend to see things only from the perspective of this natural world in which we live. As spiritual beings who have the Holy Spirit within us as our guide, teacher, and counselor, we can learn to see things from a different dimension, the spiritual dimension.

Euclid spoke to us about points, lines, planes, and parallel lines. Jesus has gone before us point by point to lay out a line of salvation in Him. Those points become a line that is continual between Jesus and our lives in Him. His line speaks, and so we are to speak words that line up with His Word. As we do this, we grow, mature, and begin to experience things in the spiritual dimension as we see the greater things of the spiritual realm displace the lesser things of the natural realm. Because Euclid spoke of parallel lines, we should be reminded that the Holy Spirit provides that parallel hedge of protection around us as we continue to move in a linear progression to the promised rest in Jesus.

After many years in Christian Radio and sports broadcasting, Todd followed God's leading start and pastor City on a Hill Teaching Center, Perrysburg, Ohio. He and his wife of 39 years, Donna, reside in Grand Rapids, Ohio.

A Founding Era Sermon That Has Applications for Today

Scriptural Instructions To Civil Leaders

Excerpts from Samuel Sherwood's Message in 1774

David, who had, for many years, exercised an absolute sovereignty and dominion over the Kingdom of Israel, had no notion of aggrandizing himself and his nobility, by enslaving his subjects and stripping them of their property, at his own arbitrary will and pleasure, contrary to law and right: but considered himself as appointed to serve them, whose rights and privileges were esteemed by him, more sacred and inviolable than those of the royal scepter and diadem…

When civil rulers, forgetting the end of their institution and the proper duties of their station, neglect and trample upon the rules of justice and consult only to gratify their own pride and ambitious humour and passion: when they consider their subjects as an inferior species of beings, made as beast of burden, for their pleasure or profit; when, instead of observing the reason and nature of things, they make their own mere will and pleasure, the rule of acting; and govern in an arbitrary, tyrannical manner; 'tis impossible to describe the evils and mischiefs they bring on mankind.…

…if they have no fear and dread on their minds, of appearing before, and accounting to their supreme judge, the sovereign ruler of the world; they will be in the utmost danger, not only of ruining themselves both for time and eternity but also, of ruining their subjects…

We want wise, steady, judicious rulers in such a day as this; men of sterling integrity and real religion… Blessed are the people that are under his care and conduct; yea, blessed are the people whose God is the Lord. Amen.

The Lord IS My Shepherd

By Vonda Hogle

Do you have certain scriptures that are your "go to" when you are feeling overwhelmed or anxious? I think the one passage that a lot of people at least reference in their mind, even if it is not necessarily a life verse, is Psalm 23. Next to John 3:16, these are probably the most quoted verses – at least in Western culture. Even if people don't know the actual address of the verses, they are familiar with the verbiage. Movies and television shows will use this passage, and it has even made its way into secular song lyrics. We hear it so much that it almost becomes common, and we miss so much of the richness of this short, six verse chapter.

If you were in church any time before the 1990s, chances are you learned this passage from the King James Version:

23 The Lord is my Shepherd; I shall not want.

² He maketh me to lie down in green pastures: he leadeth me beside the still waters.
³ He restoreth my soul: he leadeth me in the paths of righteousness for his name's sake.
⁴ Yea, though I walk through the valley of the shadow of death, I will fear no evil: for thou art with me; thy rod and thy staff they comfort me.
⁵ Thou preparest a table before me in the presence of mine enemies: thou anointest my head with oil; my cup runneth over.
⁶ Surely goodness and mercy shall follow me all the days of my life: and I will dwell in the house of the Lord forever.

The old English almost makes you feel as though you can picture it in a Peter Jackson depiction of a J.R.R. Tolkien novel. The lush rolling hills and teaming streams come to a place of stillness. The valley of the shadow of death looks like a place that you may run to in order to escape the orcs or goblins. Can you picture the table that the Lord would prepare in the presence of our enemies – the grandness of it all?

However, if we look at David's point of reference as he wrote this psalm, having been a shepherd and now seeing himself as a sheep, the picture looks totally different. To help us gain some understanding, I am going to bring in some other translations as we look at this passage verse by verse.

At the start, David states what his position is in relationship to the Lord. "The Lord," he says, "is my shepherd…" To David, this had great significance because he had been a shepherd. He knew that as a shepherd, he was responsible for every aspect of the sheep's life – to feed them, keep them safe, provide and protect them from predators and even themselves at times. So, by making this statement, he is admitting submission and the need for the Lord to take care of him.

Why is that significant? It is because by the time he wrote this psalm, he had not just been a shepherd, but a protector having killed wild beasts; a warrior, having killed a giant and saving the troop of Israel; a leader, having led troops into battle; and a king who ruled over a nation. He was in the highest position of authority, with many people relying on him and looking to him for comfort, leadership, and protection, yet he likens himself to a sheep, a very lowly animal that is totally reliant on someone else for their care. David knew his place, and without the provision and relationship with the Lord, he could not have achieved or done anything for the people he was leading. Drawing from that shepherding experience, David knew that providing for sheep was no easy feat. He had to know where to take the sheep so that they would have plenty to eat and drink. This meant knowing the lay of the land and what predators inhabited it, and their habits so he could protect his flock. He had to keep track of each and every one, no matter how big or small it was, giving an account for each and every one. David had seen God do these things in his life over and over again, providing from the time he was a shepherd boy all alone protecting his father's flock to when he was King over a powerful nation and all the steps between to get him there. How the Lord did this is revealed throughout the passage.

We tend to gloss over this with the thought of a shepherd being someone who just walked next to a herd of sheep and got them to a place that they could just eat and rest, not understanding how much work goes into herding and protecting them. When we do that, we can't fully understand how the Lord takes care of us. Verse 2 says, *"He maketh me lay down in green pastures: he leadeth me beside still waters."* Quite a picture. When my mother passed away, our family received three blankets with the 23rd Psalm on them, and all of them portrayed a field, a green, verdant field where the sheep didn't even have to bend down to eat because the clover was at mouth height. I can guarantee that was not the picture in David's mind as he wrote those words.

The pastures that David would have led his sheep in were nothing like we think of here in our culture. Our point of reference would be something you would drive past on our farm, an agriculturally rich countryside, but that is not what it would have looked like in Israel. The pastures that David was familiar with would have likely been on a hill or steep incline and would have looked pretty barren and arid with rocks every few feet. Their yearly precipitation is at least a foot less than we experience annually and mostly concentrated between December and February, leaving three-quarters of the year with the challenge of having enough water to support their agriculture.

A green pasture to the shepherds of Israel isn't what we would call green, but they can see the green in areas that would appear barren to us. Moisture is picked up off the surrounding bodies of water and blows across the hills, where it is then deposited on the rocks. On the sides of the rocks that face the water, there are tufts of grass and vegetation that grow, creating areas of green every few feet.

Shepherds look for these green pastures and lead their sheep there to graze and get their fill. To graze on this terrain, the sheep go from rock to rock, getting the mouthful of greens that form there, then off to the next mouthful. They don't get their entire feeding done in a two-foot square space where they just need to move their necks to their next bite. These sheep have to keep moving toward the next bite. The Shepherd doesn't have them all lie down to serve them. They are active participants in their feeding. Then, when they have all eaten, he takes them to a place to just rest.

So, how does the Lord lead us to green pastures? Well, the pasture is the sustenance for the sheep – the nutrients that are essential for them to live. He has also given us a source for sustenance, and to be honest, ours does look more like the green pastures from the blanket I got at my mom's funeral. We are fortunate to live in a place where we have access to the Word of God, like no other. I am almost ashamed of how many Bibles I have in my home, a lot of which I don't read daily because I do so on a phone, tablet, or computer. There are Bible studies, sermons, and podcasts where we can gorge ourselves on what God is telling us, but – we are still like the sheep. We have to make the effort to get from one mouthful to the next.

Let's be honest – at times in my life, I spend time in God's word like I'm at a huge family dinner with unending bowls of whatever I want to eat, and I spend time taking it in and discussing things with those at the table, too. Other times, I am going from mouthful to mouthful, trusting that God is going to speak to me right where I am. I might not spend as much time sitting down and reading, but I am listening to it in my car between appointments. In either situation, my Shepherd makes sure that there is enough for what I need – I just need to walk to that next rock.

Then there is the part about Him making us lie down, resting, and slowing down by still waters. The New Living Translation says, "peaceful waters."

As I was growing up, there were some things that were just a part of our Sunday experience. We went to church every Sunday morning, and because my mother was always involved in ministry in one way or another, we were there early and usually were the ones locking up the building. Then, we got to go out to eat. This may seem extravagant, but my single mother worked all week long, then poured herself out on Sunday morning, so this was her one indulgence. Then, when we got home, without fail, we all took a nap. This wasn't a "lie down for a few minutes and rest" kind of nap. This was a "strip down to your slip and crawl back into bed" kind of nap. We slept on Sunday afternoons without the distraction of TVs, computers, tablets, or phones. My mother, as she shepherded us, made us lie down by peaceful waters.

I believe the Lord provides those times for us, too, but too many times, we don't recognize them, or we fill that space with other things. We bring our phone, tablet or computer with us. We can't stay off social media long enough to take in the rest that God desires for us to have – time to truly meditate on what He is feeding us and speaking to us. We are also good at masking our inability to rest by demonstrating what we are hearing from the Lord by posting a verse or passage on Facebook or Instagram. That doesn't count, and it never impresses God.

Verse 3 says, *"He restoreth my soul: he leadeth me in the paths of righteousness for his name's sake."* What does it mean to "restoreth my soul"? The dictionary defines it as "to bring back to or put back into a former or original state".

Do you remember what it was like when you first started your relationship with the Lord? Or maybe it took a while for you to really trust and completely experience His love and goodness for you. When we are in that place, we tend to stand on the scripture and promises of God with more confidence and rest in who He is and who He says we are. However, over time, day-to-day life tends to set in and chip away at that confidence, that reliance; and we allow doubt to creep in or rely on our own strength to accomplish and dictate what we do. God doesn't want us to stay there, or even worse, continue down that path. His desire is to continually bring us back into a relationship with Him of trust and love and allow it to grow in more depth.

In The New Living Translation, the second part of the verse says, *"He guides me along right paths, bringing honor to his name."*

Recently I was traveling with a friend who didn't know how to get to the exact location we were going but knew part of the way there. I punched in the destination address on Google Maps, and we headed on our way. At one point, the navigation told me to turn down a country road, but my friend insisted that we keep going straight for another mile or so, then turn. This turn took us into a little town, and the speed limit decreased greatly, slowing us down. This road took us through neighborhoods and on twists and turns before heading back out on a two-lane country road. On my way home, I decided to go the way that the navigation had instructed. Rather than going through neighborhoods or the small town, it took us on a much faster route and allowed us to keep our speed with only two turns.

"Just like sheep, sometimes when we go our own way to get to where we are going, we go through things we could avoid if we would just follow the Shepherd."

While forging our own way, we may run into things that slow us down or could even delay us from getting to where God has planned for us. When we listen for His voice, His direction, the end of our journey, whether it is the one of our complete life or one of the many journeys He takes us on throughout life, will testify of His goodness, protection and provision. When we don't follow His voice and direction, the testimony centers more around how He has saved us from our own poor choices.

In The New International Version, verse 4 says, *"Even though I walk through the darkest valley, I will fear no evil, for you are with me; your rod and your staff, they comfort me."* There is so much in this one verse.

First, it doesn't say that we may or may not encounter dark valleys – even the darkest valley. It says even though I do. I know many people who are the first to tell you how great

God is when everything is going their way, but at the first sign of trouble, they begin to question if He is there or if He even cares. We are not promised a life exempt from trouble. We are promised that just like a shepherd doesn't leave his flock when he senses danger but stays with them, guiding them through and fighting to protect them, the Lord is with us. He is not sitting in heaven watching us struggle wondering how we are going to make it. He is Emmanuel, God with us – fully aware of what we are experiencing and facing and preparing our way through it with His protection.

His provision and protection sometimes are not realized at the time. When we look at the tools the Shepherd uses, they sound harsh – a rod and a staff – but they both have important roles in getting the sheep to where they are going safely.

The rod is made from a large piece of wood and usually has a knob at one end. When using it defensively, the Shepherd will throw it at a predator to either injure or kill it or at the least scare it away. It can also be used when one sheep is heading off on its own. The Shepherd will throw the rod on the far side of the wayward sheep to corral it back with the herd.

Have you ever been following what you know God has called you to do, and you come up against opposition? Then, without you having to do anything, the problem goes away or resolves itself? That is our Shepherd throwing the rod at the enemy. Or, have you started to do something that may be just a little off what God told you? It's no big deal and not going to hurt anything when all of a sudden, the thing you were about to do either is no longer appealing or rejects you? He is using that rod to cut you off from veering away from His plan.

The staff has a long reach and is hooked at the end. Most of us can picture a shepherd using it to hook around the neck of a sheep that is leaving and has gotten farther away than is safe to throw the rod as a distraction. The staff can reach the sheep in places that it may have gone that are too small for the Shepherd to squeeze into to retrieve it. The hook may seem like a harsh way to pull the sheep back, but the Shepherd knows that to get its compliance, he needs to place the hook around the sheep's chin and bottom jaw and gently guide its head in the direction it needs to go.

I think this is one of God's favorite things to use as He shepherds us. When we are going in the wrong direction, He uses so many things to gently bring us back to where we need to be. It could be anything from the word of admonition from a trusted person in our lives to a lyric in a song that reminds us of who we are and what we should be doing.

At the end of the hook on a staff, it curves back up and makes another little hook going the opposite direction. At night, shepherds can stand the staff upright in the ground and hang a lantern on the little hook so he can see the sheep and so the sheep can know where he is. Our Shepherd does the same thing. Even at our lowest and darkest place, we can always know where He is because His promises are the light of hope to see us through our situations.

The last two verses of this psalm change its vantage point from looking at the Lord as our Shepherd to one who hosts us. *"You prepare a table before me in the presence of my enemies. You anoint my head with oil; my cup overflows."* (verse 5) This verse shifts our view from being metaphorical in an intangible way – we are not going to be actual sheep – to metaphors that also could translate literally.

I have always been a bit puzzled by the Lord preparing a table, or as other translations say, a feast, in the presence of those I may be in strife with or literally opposed to. For most of my life in my mind, I could see myself perched at the head of a table with everything delicious spread out before me; and watching my enemies' mouths water as they watch me consume whatever and as much as I want without allowing them to have anything. Nana nana boo boo! Recently, though, as I was reading Jeremiah 29, my understanding has changed.

In Jeremiah 29, the Lord has a word for those who were exiled from Jerusalem to Babylon. We like to quote verse 11 that says that He has great plans for their, and our, lives – for a hope and a future. We are not as quick to quote verses 5-7, *"Build houses and settle down; plant gardens and eat what they produce. Marry and have sons and daughters; find wives for your sons and give your daughters in marriage, so that they too may have sons and daughters. Increase in number there; do not decrease. Also, seek the peace and prosperity of the city to which I have carried you into exile. Pray to the Lord for it, because if it prospers, you too will prosper."*

Wait, is that right? God wanted those in exile to not only settle in but seek peace and prosperity for the city of Babylon? Really? Then he hits them with the paradox – "Pray to the Lord for it because if it prospers, you too will prosper."

So, knowing the nature of God and that He is not haughty, I don't think He would set us up with a banquet table just to flaunt it before our enemies. What I think He would do is set us up to host our enemy and show them the goodness of our God, giving them an invitation to come join us and introduce them to the One who provides it all.

The next part of the verse speaks to how the Lord covers us with His presence. In the Old Testament, anointing someone with oil was a demonstration of God's favor and identification of the one He had chosen. For us, it represents God's presence in our lives and that we are each chosen by Him. It is by His presence that we have all that we need in any circumstance.

When David wrote this, he understood the significance of the anointing on a person's head as a symbol of God choosing him; but I believe David was also considering how shepherds anoint their sheep's heads with oil, as well. Shepherds take oil and rub it all around the sheep's eyes and ears because of the species of flies that would be drawn to and gather in those places. As the flies go into their eyes, they not only irritate them but can spread conjunctivitis, or pink eye, which becomes highly contagious and impairs their vision. These flies also make their way into the ears of the sheep and will lay eggs. This can cause problems from clogging their ear canals to the larva boring into their brain and causing them to go mad. When the Shepherd coats the eyes and ears with oil, it provides a layer of protection so that the flies cannot make contact with the skin of the sheep in these vulnerable places.

Still recognizing that the Lord is our Shepherd, His presence – His anointing – is that protection we need from allowing the enemy to attack us in the vulnerable places of what and how we see and hear things, as well as guarding our minds.

When we truly consider all that the Lord has done and continues to do for us, we do not have the capacity to contain it, and it should flow out from us. It's like when a cup cannot contain what is being poured into it, what is being poured in will spill out on all sides.

This brings us to the end of the chapter – verse 6 *"Surely your goodness and unfailing love will pursue me all the days of my life, and I will live in the house of the Lord forever."* (NLT) David created this whole psalm to illustrate God's goodness towards us and buttons it up with such a great promise.

Surely – confidently, with certainty. David trusted his Shepherd to the point that he could say, without question, that the things he had experienced in his life would not end, but was the foundation of his life that everything rested on. I love the way he sums it up, knowing that the goodness of God would not just be available to him and to us, but it pursues us. The song by Cory Asbury says it so well: "…it chases me down, fights 'til I'm found, leaves the ninety-nine … the overwhelming, never-ending, reckless love of God." (Reckless Love) Though we may choose to turn away or not accept it, God's action doesn't change. He pursues us because of His love for us. It doesn't hinge on our actions, beliefs, or decisions.

I can't say what "living in the house of the Lord" meant to David personally, but I believe it to be prophetic for us in our day. Jesus told us about it in John 14:2-3 *"My Father's house has many rooms; if that were not so, would I have told you that I am going there to prepare a place for you?³ And if I go and prepare a place for you, I will come back and take you to be with me that you also may be where I am."* This is the promise that we have to spend eternity with God in the physical, but in 1 Corinthians 6:19, Paul also tells us that we, ourselves, are the house of the Lord *"Do you not know that your bodies are temples of the Holy Spirit, who is in you, whom you have received from God?"* We are the house of the Lord – our physical being – and that cannot be taken away. I think of what a comfort that is to those believers who live in areas of the world where going to a house of worship is not just against the law, but it is also dangerous. They are the house of the Lord. His presence resides and occupies their, and our, very being. What an amazing promise.

David expressed his experience of life in relationship with the Lord by likening it to what he knew at his very core – how to be a good shepherd. As you reflect on this psalm, I hope that looking at it through his experience and perspective gives you some more depth and understanding of what David was meaning to convey about his Lord. And, if you are up for the challenge, how would you write a psalm of how you view your relationship with God-given your experience and perspective?

Vonda is the mother to two amazing daughters and has had the privilege of being involved in ministry, locally and internationally. She is on staff at Vineyard Church and works with Keep Watch, working to see every school covered in prayer, so the power and presence of God are experienced in our communities.

Marriage Proverbs for 2022
Cultivate Strong Roots for Your Marriage

You have the opportunity to be the greatest witness of Jesus your
spouse will ever see. Make the most of the opportunity each day.

Listen to your spouse more than you speak. You will learn to hear
the Lord speaking His wisdom through them to you.

Don't compare your husband or wife with the husband or wife of others. Not only is this
not wise, it can also blind you to the unique beauty that Jesus created in your own marriage.

When you know with certainty that you are right, be open to the possibility
that you may actually be wrong. Then ask the Holy Spirit to reveal the truth.

Read the Word together, pray together, and talk about Jesus together. You are one in Him.

Complaining about things costs you nothing, and you get what you pay for, nothing.
Results demand a sacrifice. Instead of being quick to complain, be quick to find resolutions.

If you want to strengthen your marriage, strive to be the person they cannot live without.

What you take for granted today creates the possible reality that it may not be there tomorrow.
Therefore, always appreciate what God has given you in marriage.

Marriage requires work and effort. But never forget that marriage is also supposed
to be fun and joyous. So let the joy of the Lord flow through your oneness.

An Extraordinary Life

By Linda Cunning, Ph.D.

Have you ever stared at something ordinary? You see it every day, but a day comes and you take notice of the ordinary. The more you observe, experiment, take apart, the more you realize the ordinary is extraordinary. The revelation of the extraordinary can be life-changing.

That happened to me. An ordinary object that I used and abused became this extraordinary subject of study. Practically speaking, I think they look odd. Why would God make them in this way? Each of the five extensions does not match. They are different sizes. The bottom seems like it should be straight, but when it is straight, it causes problems. Large and small connectors provide stability, strength, and agility. The wrapping is actually different textures depending upon where it is located around the connectors. The individuality of the owner comes into play when you see what is painted or attached or wrapped around it. This mode of transportation is immensely valuable. You would not even know how valuable because it is so ordinary. Until something is wrong.

It was late, but I wanted to get one more thing done before going to bed. I grabbed the electric drill and an old ladder that I had for years, and before that, my mother used. As I reached to drill the hole for the curtain rod cradle, the ladder came out from under me, and the drill hit my foot as we both collapsed to the ground. So, I laid there, stunned from the fall, looking down to see the damage.

The ordinary of a scripture in which you have read over and over becomes extraordinary when you see the scripture differently. You may have read a scripture over and over, but a time comes, maybe you prayed for illumination, and suddenly, this time, the scripture comes alive, relevant, extraordinary. *He set my feet on a rock* (Psalm 40:2) explains the importance of a life given to God. An old ladder is like an old life. I am not talking just about a life without Christ. I am talking about a life that truly has not given God the chance to take the controls and lead this life as He desires to lead it. Like the old ladder, this old life cannot sustain you for long before you tumble. Psalm 40 explains that God is taking you out of the mire. Mire is that slippery, slimy muck that is so hard to walk in. You can't move forward without great effort. If the muck is too thick, you get stuck. Interesting. In the muck, in the times of pain,

in times of trying to do life in our own way, if we release our own agenda and wait patiently to hear and obey the Lord, this action grabs His attention. He turns towards you and lifts you out to put those two feet on the rock. His rock is a firm foundation.

Selah moment: Where do you feel stuck in the mire of your life's circumstances? How can you release it to God? How can you wait so the Lord can come to lift you out of the mire?

Once I hit the ground, I looked down toward my foot and saw before my eyes the ankle balloon. I mean, the swelling was so immediate, I thought, "this cannot be for real." I blinked my eyes again. I did not feel the pain at first, but I was completely unable to move my foot. No up, no down. No side to side. I definitely could not put weight on it. I called out. "Hey, alexa, call 911". The round AI speaker said, "You need to use your phone for emergencies." Well, that was no help.

There are beautiful verses in Psalms that the writer is encouraging himself with the promises of God. In one particular verse, you hear the psalmist's heart-cry that he is lonely and afflicted. Psalm 25:15 and Psalm 31:8 are examples of this. Specifically, in verse 15, *My eyes are ever on the Lord, for only He will release my feet from the snare.* Have you ever been in a place in which troubles surround you? You are scared or confused. Maybe you are angry because you see no help in sight. It is so lonely that even when you look for help, there is none. That is the place when you rehearse the promises of God. The psalmist pronounces, "My eyes are ever on the Lord..." As you walk through those tough days, those lonely nights, and those stormy seasons, it is the Lord that breaks you free so your feet are released to continue your life's journey. When you and I focus on the Father, God frees us within the circumstances. The circumstance may not change immediately, or the answer or the conclusion may not be immediate. But the peace of God that supersedes our own understanding of the situation reassures us that God's release, His freedom is here. We can walk in confidence that the Father has released us from the snare.

Selah moment: Think of a recent time when you took your eyes off the Lord. What "snare," like in the scripture, could God have saved you the heartache or trouble if you were to have kept your eyes on Him?

What is interesting about the words foot and feet is that it is referenced in the King James Version of the bible 241 times. In scripture, if something is important, it is referenced often. So, seeing that feet are so important and repeated throughout scripture, we would want to know why. Feet correlate to multiple Biblical themes. The foot could represent walking the path of the new birth in Christ, protection from this world's evil, cleansing of the soul, worship to God, to sever from, taking territory, instructions, serving, and ministry. These many scriptures all have something in common. There is movement. There is an action. Something does or will happen.

Our feet, in the spirit, take us on adventures. How we approach each adventure can determine its outcome. Ruth is an excellent example of this adventure. A young widow, she could easily have returned to her familiar people and ways of life that she knew, but her husband and his family impacted her so much that her feet followed Naomi into the unknown. Ruth said to Naomi, "…your God is my God." She had no idea the adventure that awaited her as she loved God and loved Naomi. Fast forward, and a man named Boaz was a relation to Naomi. Wealthy and kind, Naomi knew this was a match made in Heaven. Literally. Ruth has been in Boaz's fields gleaning for food. At that time, it was customary for the landowner to protect his grain from theft by spending the night on the threshing floor. Naomi gives Ruth these instructions. "Tonight, he *(Boaz)* will be willowing barley on the threshing floor. Wash and perfume yourself and put on your best clothes…When he lies down, go and <u>uncover his feet</u> and lie down. He will tell you what to do."

The uncovering of the feet is symbolic. If you think of the old testament references that every place you set your feet will be yours (Deuteronomy 11:24; Joshua 3:3; Psalm 8:6), Boaz exposed feet can make him either possess what is below them or be exposed to something or someone that could harm him. As a close relative to Naomi, Ruth lies below his feet in a beautiful act of humility while revealing that he, Boaz, is her kinsman-redeemer. Have you ever been in a "feet exposed" position? In a place where you humbly become a steward over something wonderful and great, or regretfully exposed to harm or sin? Sometimes it is in that place of decision in which you could go either the best of what God has for you or the path that leads to trouble and heartache. Boaz chose to act upon being the kinsman-redeemer for Ruth, even going above and beyond to make it happen. Faith walking is so much like this "feet exposing" position. But the rewards for following God's way are incredible.

Selah: When have your "feet" been exposed? What decisions did you make that impacted you positively or negatively? What "feet" figuratively have you submitted yourself to lately? What has happened because of this? How can you recognize what to submit to and what to not be exposed to?

Personally, my faith walking led me to a new state, a new church, a new town, a new job, a new everything it seemed. But I knew the scripture, *Every place where you set your feet will be yours* (Deuteronomy 11:24).

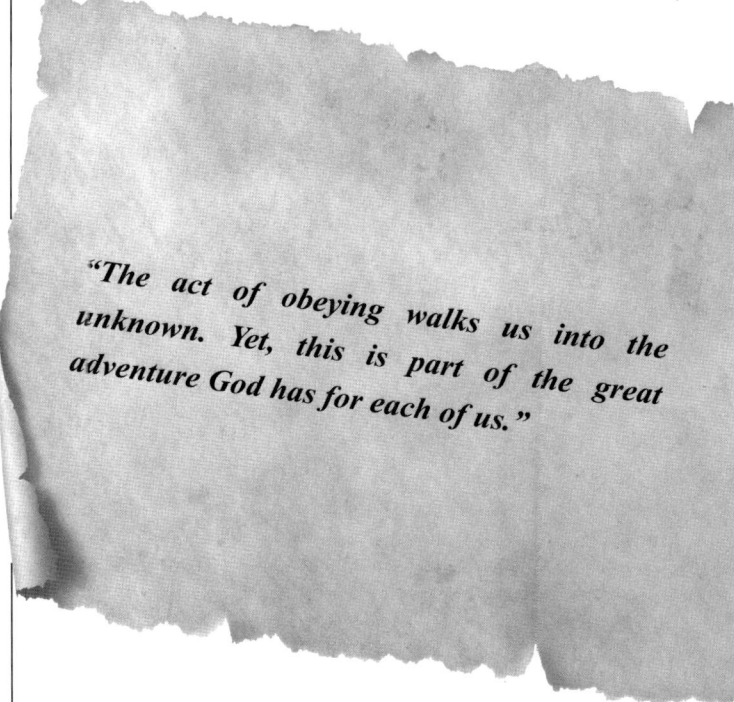

"The act of obeying walks us into the unknown. Yet, this is part of the great adventure God has for each of us."

Faith walking is a humble walk. Faith walking lets you see outside of the day-to-day ordinary and adventure into the extraordinary. If fear leads, then you miss the extraordinary moments that are life-changing. Faith walking is liberating in so many ways. What is great is that you can experience this faith walk every day.

You also serve others in this faith walk. In fact, that is what faith is for, impacting those God has placed in the path of where you are setting your feet. That is another adventure that can be scary but so fulfilling. Jesus truly set this example as He, the King of Kings, humbly washed each of the disciples' feet. If you think about it, even the person that he knew was His betrayer, Jesus held his heel in His hand, took a cloth dipped in cleansing water, and wiped the dirt from Judas' feet. Think about your daily walk. Each day, how you get up, clean up, and start your day. On the path of your daily walk, there is an opportunity for you to walk by faith. It may be a word of encouragement or maybe an act of kindness to a stranger. Walking by faith may lead you to apologize to someone who has hurt you, knowing it should be that person apologizing. The best part is that you do not expect anything in return. Faith walking is service to others while building a stronger relationship with Christ because faith pleases God (Hebrews 11:6). Humbling yourself in service to others opens ministry like no other act. This type of service brings others to the feet of God. From there, they receive council, healing, conviction, and encouragement. The love of God is truly manifested in humility. Challenge yourself to symbolically wash the feet of someone each day and watch the extraordinary happen.

Selah: This past week, how have you (symbolically) washed the feet of those you love and respect as well as those you do not like? Who have you missed or ignored that you need to go back to serve as an act of faith?

Why are feet so important? Because although feet may seem like the most unlikely hero to the body's function, feet are incredibly significant to our overall wellbeing and productivity. Your feet are the foundation for your body. They bear all of the weight. Your foot goes through a complex series of movements just for you to take a step. Think about when you have had a small piece of pebble, or stick, or any foreign object in your shoe. You are miserable until you can get it away from your foot. That dreaded blister after walking too long, oh my! What about those beautiful stilettos, those gorgeous high heels that not only are incredibly painful but can actually change the gait over time if worn too much. Not taking care of your feet leads to problems with your walk, knees, hips, and back. Although we use and abuse our feet, we need them to be as healthy as possible to continue to live a mobile and happy lifestyle.

You cannot just say to your feet, "I don't need you." That is what Paul said in describing the importance of each person in the body of Christ (I Corinthians 12:21). Although feet may be covered with socks and shoes, their significance is great, down to the last toe. Sometimes, "church folks" have a wrong impression of significance, personally and in others. We see people in terms of their professions and callings. We sometimes do not consider others as anything of importance. Maybe we ignore them altogether because we just do not see them. That is why I love how Jesus brings attention to the woman who was a widow. She was poor, but her faith walked her feet to give all she had, just two mites that were the smallest of Roman coins in that day. Jesus, watching who was giving at the temple (hmmm, interesting that He was paying attention to something people would just do, either out of obligation or to get attention). Once this woman of faith, who no one noticed, gave all that she had, Jesus called his disciples to open their eyes to see. Her. This widow. To tell them she gave more than anyone else (Mark 12:41-44).

I hate to admit this to you, but for a long time, I thought of myself as insignificant. I mean, I knew Jesus loved me, and I loved to serve others, but was I really significant to the body of believers? I felt invisible to others. So, I thought

I was insignificant. How many of us in the family of God place a value of insignificance upon ourselves? We may not be the pastor or doing full-time five-fold ministry. We may not even see that our small contributions mean anything. That is such a sad mindset to have. Long ago, I prayed to the Father to open my eyes to see others as He sees them. My goodness, what a prayer that changed my life. Each day I would look at a person and see, supernaturally, the love of the Father for him or her. I saw potential and possibility. I saw greatness and service. I saw extravagant concierge and unimaginable talents. This from people who disliked me. People who hated believers of Christ, people who were liars, connivers, and just plain evil. These people were abusers, convicts, and gossipers. But, the love of the Father of His creation changed what I thought of these people. Judgment turned because mercy triumphs over judgment (James 2:13). Each person that you see on your social media, or as you walk through the halls of school, or while you are in a meeting at work, or sitting next to in church, has significance and value. We cannot say to the feet I have no need for you. We are all here on this earth, each one created by God for a purpose. Those "feet" are priceless.

Selah: This week, pray each day for the Father to open your eyes to see the invisible people. Ask Him to help you to make them feel loved by the Father and significant. Make sure you realize your worth and significance also. You are not invisible to God.

After two surgeries, reciting healing scriptures, much time in prayer, using a knee scooter, a walker, crutches, and a cane, attending physical therapy, doing countless foot exercises, and lifestyle changes during recovery, I can happily proclaim I am walking again. Success is defined differently for each person. I take my definition from Psalm 18:33, which states, *He makes my feet like hinds' feet, He enables me to stand on the heights* (Habakkuk 3:19). This is also quoted in the beautiful and classic Christian allegory book, Hinds Feet on High Places (Hubbard, Hannah. 1979). If you have not read the book, you will enjoy it. For me, this book came at a time of tremendous struggles and heartache. The second time this book was read was to my children as we all walked through hard and dark places in our lives together. As the character, Much-Afraid walks through her journey, I could relate in so many ways. Your walk with the Lord is unique to you because God made you unique. But the experiences we go through are not unique since there are so many who have walked those same paths. I pray that you allow the Father to make your feet like hinds' feet. Those hinds' feet are designed by God to climb to the high mountains. Those hinds' feet can grab on to what seems to be the steepest stones. Those feet are beautiful because beautiful are the feet of those that bring good news (Isaiah 52:7).

This ordinary life of mine became extraordinary as I walked by faith. Although I still feel a little limp, a change in my gait, so to speak. It kind of reminds me of Jacob's limp leftover when he wrestled with God all night long. Jacob's reminder that it is not his way that matters, but God's way. You will see me walking with no limp, as I completely believe in God's healing virtue. Yet, I will not forget that thirty years prior to this life-changing accident during a life-changing faith walk, God spoke to me to study feet in the scriptures. I had no idea then that what I thought was an ordinary study would become an extraordinary reflection of my walk with the Lord.

Linda Cunning, Ph.D., is a lover of the Father, her children, the Word, worship, learning, people, writing, and faith. This love has taken her on incredible experiences in life. Her current adventure is leading an educational nonprofit and speaking and training a variety of people and groups.

Greek and Hebrew Words To Know in 2022

Memorial

The Hebrew word we read as "memorial" was often tied to things like memorial stones in the Old Testament. These would serve as a reminder of a miracle of God on behalf of His people. Those ancient memorial stones of the Bible speak to us, reminding us to be His memorial stones today. Our lives should be filled with testimonies of the faithfulness and miracles of Jesus that call the attention of the world to Jesus. Our lives should memorialize daily His covenant with us.

Knowledge

In 2 Peter, we read this: *but grow in the grace and knowledge of our Lord and Savior Jesus Christ. To Him be the glory both now and forever. Amen.* 2 Peter 3:18 NKJV

The Greek word we read as "knowledge" refers to functional or working knowledge that comes from first-hand experience. It is a knowing that comes from a direct personal relationship. Do you have the desire to receive first-hand knowledge regarding the Word of God and knowledge to apply daily in your life? Peter indicates that we can grow into this kind of eternal revelation and wisdom because of our personal relationship with Father God through Jesus! He wants to personally show you things that are otherwise unknowable, so press in and receive a working knowledge of the greater things of the kingdom of God.

Rest

By Josh Plasaince

REST - definition.
1. To refresh oneself, as by sleeping, lying down, or relaxing.
2. To relieve weariness by cessation of exercise or labor.
3. To be at ease; have tranquility or peace.
4. To be quiet or still
5. To cease from motion, come to rest; stop.
6. To become or remain inactive.

Even at the reading of the definition, one can find themselves taking deeper breaths and feeling their heart catch up with their mind. Rest is the elusive thing that so many run after, that so many desire, that so many want to experience. With this push to experience rest, it brings the questions to the surface of why does one not rest, what is the cause for the lack of rest, and how can one find rest?

As a minister of the gospel, while I find fulfillment in the call that the Lord has on my life, I also realize the need to step away from the drive of that call to take a break. It is not a throwing up of the hands and walking away, but a break to allow my mind and heart that opportunity to grow silent and refreshed. Rest can happen on vacation, but not all vacations are restful... said every dad. I have found, as I have led my church, that in my seasons of rest that it allows others the opportunity to grow and bloom in their call. There are times when the breakthrough that I have been praying for in my church happens when I am away, reminding me once again that it is not all about me.

In Genesis, we find rest as a model that so many of us go back to. God has just finished creating for six days, *"God saw all that he had made, and it was very good."* (Genesis 1:31). *"By the seventh day God had finished the work he had been doing; so on the seventh day he rested from all his work. Then God blessed the seventh day and made it holy, because on it he rested from all the work of creating that he had done."* (Genesis 2:2-3) To stop and think about an all-present God taking a rest because what He had already accomplished was good, how do we justify our constant push forward to accomplish more and fill more time?

At the core of rest, one has to decide that they want to care for themselves; physically, emotionally, and spiritually.

"Rest, while it can often be overlooked, is one of the most important elements of self-growth."

Speaking from experience, without the intentionality of planning for rest in my own life, rest will not happen. There should be nobody else that is pushing for me and cares for the state of my being more than myself.

As we journey through the Old Testament, we find that when Moses met with God and gave him the Ten Commandments, that the fourth One covered the plan of rest and sabbath.

"Remember the sabbath day, to keep it holy. Six days you shall labor and do all your work, but the seventh day is a sabbath of the Lord your God; in it, you shall not do any work, you or your son or your daughter, you male or your female servant or your cattle or your sojourner who stays with you. For in six days, the Lord made the heavens and the earth, the sea and all that is in them, and rested on the seventh day; therefore the Lord blessed the sabbath day and made it holy." Exodus 20:6-11

God begins this commandment with the word, 'remember" which takes them back to the days before they were captive in Egypt. This reminder was to refresh the importance of the sabbath in one's life and that it was not something new, but yet it was something that was to be practiced all along. The reason why they were unable to practice the sabbath rest was the fact that they lacked religious understanding while they were being held captive in Egypt.

The fourth commandment is an important reminder but also an important step in our journey to serve the Lord. We have six days that we are able to do whatever we want with our bodies and work, but the seventh day is the day that we give back to the Lord. In the six days, there is a planning and prep for the seventh day's arrival. Wood, food, and any other thing that would take away from worshipping the Lord would have been prepped and ready to go so that when the day of rest arrived, the individual could fully devote their day to honoring the Lord.

Beyond rest, we see that there is a joy and satisfaction

in what had been accomplished in the prior six days. In creation, it was an opportunity for God to step back and look at all that He had done and to take joy in the work that He did. In our lives, we have the opportunity to look back and not only see what we have accomplished but also to take that day and remind ourselves of our inability to accomplish all that without the power and presence of God in our lives.. There is a place of joy within us that joins with the psalmist, "For you, O Lord, you have made me glad by what You have done, I will sing for joy at the works of Your hands." Psalm 92:4

Sabbath rest is not just an Old Testament mandate, but One that is for today. Matthew records in his gospel, *"Come to Me, all who are weary and heavy-laden, and I will give you rest. Take My yoke upon you and learn from Me, for I am gentle and humble in heart, and you will find rest for your souls. For My yoke is easy and My burden is light."* (Matthew 11:28-30) As Jesus speaks to the crowds, the word is being relayed to John, who was imprisoned. "Come to Me..." the One you call healer, the One who provides, the One who serves as our advocate.

The beginning of you and I finding rest takes place when we leave where we are and come to Jesus. The act of coming to Jesus forces us to take our eyes off ourselves and our situation and directs our eyes towards Him. Jesus is the One who was there in the beginning, the One who walked the face of the earth, and the One who is preparing a place for you and I, where we will spend eternity. There is a place of hope in His name. There is a drawing in when His name is spoken. There is peace when we invite Him into our lives and our situations. When He is lifted up, He will draw all men to Himself (John 12:32).

What a Savior! What a rescuer! What a healer! What peace!

"All" (in Matthew 11:28) means you, me, your neighbor, your spouse, all! We are all welcome at the feet of Jesus. Are you "weary and heavy-laden"? There is good news for you too... He welcomes you. Bring your burdens, bring your baggage, bring your needs, bring your sin to Him. The invitation that Jesus is giving is not limited by what you are carrying and what is weighing you down, but it is an open invitation that no matter what you see in the natural, or what you are feeling in emotions, or what you are carrying spiritually, He is waiting for you to come to Him.

Picture yourself walking through the door after a crazy, busy day, and your roommate, spouse, special someone is there cooking an amazing meal. You are hit with a majestic smell as the door opens. If you are blessed enough, you may even have smelled the aromas even before you opened the door. As you walk in, take off your shoes, hang up your keys, and lay down your bag, there is a sigh of relief that comes from within, "I have made it home." With your head up, you walk around the corner to see a lovely meal laid out and ready for you to enjoy.

This picture is the picture of what Jesus is saying to you and me as we come to Him weary and heavy-laden. We may be worn out from the day that we have been through, but there Jesus is. He has prepared a place for you because He was expecting you. He knew you were coming. He was waiting for you to walk through that door. In a world that displays Jesus as far away, out of reach, and out of touch, to know that He is prepared and ready for you can in itself release the pressure and weights that you are carrying. What a Savior!

Stop for a moment and just picture that scene... picture yourself walking through the door and laying everything down... now lift your head and see Jesus. He is standing there, ready for you. He was expecting you.

To some, just the simple image of Jesus standing there and expecting you is so overwhelming. There is something amazing that is happening at this moment that goes beyond the "stuff" that you carried into the room. That "stuff" has so little value and weight compared to seeing Jesus... and knowing that He was waiting for you.

None of us are short in the weary and heavy-laden category. We all have burdens and weights that we carry that limit and steal the peace that we have in our lives. The real question that we have to ask ourselves is, do we want to hold onto all of that, or are we willing to let it go? Real peace, real rest, will only come to us as we come to Jesus and lay all of this weight at His feet.

Just as He started this verse focused on Himself, He ends the same way with the ability to find rest in Him. I believe it is telling of our situations and the heaviness that we carry that Jesus needs to remind us again in the same verse that He is the One who is able to take care of all of our needs. In our self-sufficient view, promoted by the world, we find it hard at times to let go and let God.

If we were to step back and look at our lives, we would see the things that keep us up at night, that are constantly sitting there in the back of our minds, waiting for us to take action. How many of those things, if we are honest with ourselves, are we able to attribute to our own picking up and our own carrying? We need to recognize that we are carrying loads that Jesus never intended for us to carry. That is where the importance of this single verse and the reminder of Jesus comes to us in that we need to make a straight line to Him and off-load these things at His feet.

Some of the items that we are carrying may be personal baggage from our past. It may be emotional baggage of what someone has done to us that we have been carrying that wrong for years. We may even be carrying sin that has been hidden deep in our lives that we are unwilling to face because we do not want to face the potential consequences. Each of these weights pushes us down and hinders the plan, call, and purpose of God in our lives. Merely the fact of us being slowed down should cause us to be willing to come to the foot of the cross and lay down our burdens.

The foot of the cross is level. Any person, from any background, with any color of skin and any amount in their bank account can come to Jesus. The foot of the cross is level, and there is not anything that you are carrying or burdened with that has not found light, hope, freedom, peace, and rest at the cross.

As we look at the remainder of the verses here in Matthew 11:29-30, we see the importance of Jesus in the process of finding peace and rest in our lives. The initial action on our side was to come to Jesus, but the second action for us is to "take." Not only do we find ourselves at the foot of the cross laying down our burdens, but when we get up, what do we do next? To some, there is the desire to pick up that which was laid down and carry it again because that is what we normally do and have been doing for a while, but here we see Jesus telling us to "take His yoke."

His yoke is not the yoke of the world, but His yoke is one of peace, one of hope, one of positioning ourselves close to Him. It is the action of us hitching ourselves to His wagon and letting Him lead us in this life. By taking His yoke, we brand ourselves as one of His while also committing to the fact that we are relinquishing our desires as we take on His plan and His heart.

As we take His yoke upon ourselves, we then find ourselves under His leadership and direction in our lives as we learn from Him. This is what happens to an ox that is yoked to a wagon, in that they learn how the owner/farmer will lead them. The mentality of learning from Jesus as we take upon our lives His yoke causes us to retrain our mind and to rewire our hearts. This is a crucial part of our finding peace and rest in our lives. When we are yoked with Jesus, we are not pulling the wagon by ourselves anymore.

The rest that He promises is deeper than the physical needs that we have in our lives. It goes down to the depth of our souls. Our body consists of three parts; the body (our flesh), soul (mind, will, and emotions), and spirit (spirit man within). While our spirit is alive in Him as we see Him working in our lives, and our body (flesh) is tired from all the physical labor that it has been doing. He is bringing peace and rest to our souls.

It must be said that in the equation of the three parts of our body, that when you and I take upon our lives His yoke, we are bringing our body (flesh) into alignment with Him. That is the purpose of the physical yoke. I know that you have heard the story of the child that was instructed to stand in class and did not want to, but when challenged, he finally did. His response was, "I may be standing on the outside, but I am sitting on the inside."

This battle within our soul, mind, will, and emotions is one that cannot just be contained and stopped from the outside. It is one that has to go deeper in impacting the way we think, the desires we have, and how we emotionally respond to the whole thing. Jesus is reminding us in this passage that He wants the rest of our lives to go to the deepest part of our being. When we process in our mind, we process from a place that is yoked to Him physically and think of the freedom and joy that comes from being completely surrendered to Him.

He not only works in our minds, but He trains us and shows us how to respond emotionally to all that we are facing. You may find yourself in an emotional basket case at times, but with His yoke upon you, you can find rest and peace from the very core of who you are. When you are not emotionally drained because of all the weight that you are carrying, having laid it at the foot of the cross, imagine the peace that you will feel and the pause that will come in your spirit as you know one additional battle does not have to be fought.

I believe that the greatest work that will come as you follow and submit yourself to Him will be the changing of your desires. What once was an overwhelming pull towards the things of this world will begin to shift towards not only a full surrender to Him but also a place of joy, peace, and rest.

To sum up the power of taking on His yoke, I am reminded of what He wants to do in our lives, from one of my life-verses, Romans 12:1-2 *"Therefore, I urge you, brothers and sisters, in view of God's mercy, to offer your bodies as a living sacrifice, holy and pleasing to God - this is your true and proper worship. Do not conform to the pattern of this world, but be transformed by the renewing of your mind. Then you will be able to test and approve what God's will is - his good, pleasing, and perfect will."*

To know the "good, pleasing and perfect," will of God for your life is one of the greatest benefits of fully coming to Him and taking upon your life His yoke. The whole trajectory of your life changes when you not only follow His Word but you apply it to your life. This is not new and not something that is so far reached that you and I cannot accomplish in our lives. In fact, it is so important that we should strive to see it fully come to pass in our own lives.

Speaking of our own lives, even at the writing of this article, I have been praying and asking the Holy Spirit to guide me in my writing. This is not just another collection of words from a pastor/Christian leader, but I believe that just as I desire to experience the rest that comes from Him, so do you. Together, we can not only see this peace and rest in our lives but also that it can serve as a hope for others as they see us walk out our faith in Christ.

Let me finish with verse 30, *'For my yoke is easy, and my burden is light.'* While I know that this is true, I also know that it will take some work on my side. I am so thankful for the love of God that He carries us through, and He gives us a way out.

Let me encourage you to stop fighting and struggling as you carry His yoke upon your shoulders. The yoke is meant to be sturdy and stiff, not conforming to your body, but for you to conform to it. As you completely surrender to Him, may you see the fruit of your surrendered life come to pass. I pray that the days become easier and lighter as you carry His yoke and you learn to trust Him more.

Rest is possible. Peace is attainable. Jesus is here… What yoke are you going to carry?

Josh Plaisance is married to Stacey and has three children. Originally from Wisconsin, he and Stacey now reside in Kettering, Ohio. Josh pastors Kettering Assembly of God. Currently, he is a Master's Student, working towards a Master's of Arts in Christian Leadership Church Planter degree. Josh is also the founder of Joshua 1:9 Ministries

Notable Events in the 22nd Year of Previous Centuries

1922

U.S. President Warren G Harding signs a joint resolution establishing a Jewish Homeland in the ancient region of Israel.

1822

Harriet Tubman who led so many enlaved African Americans to freedom through the Underground Railroad, was born. A French scholar Jean-François Champollion publishes his work on deciphering the Rosetta Stone. The beginning of understanding Egyptian hieroglyphs.

1722

On Easter Sunday Dutch explorer Jacob Roggeveen discovers a Polynesian Island off the coast of South America and names it Easter Island.

1622

Plymouth Colony settlers William Bradford and Edward Winslow wrote their account of the Colony's first year

1522

Martin Luther translates the New Testament into German making the Word of God available to the masses. Ferdinand Magellan's remaining crew arrives back in Spain completing the first circumnavigation of the earth.

1422

In Florence Italy, the Urbino Bible, considered an artistic masterpiece is produced.

1222

The Fifth Crusade ends in failure leaving Egypt in Muslim control.

722 BC

The Northern kingdom of Israel falls to the Assyrians. Fulfilling God's prophecy against them because they had gone after false gods

My Sheep Hear My Voice

By Misty Smith

27My sheep hear my voice, and I know them, and they follow me. 28I give them eternal Life, and they will never perish, and no one will snatch them out of my hand. 29My Father, who has given them to me,[a] is greater than all, and no one is able to snatch them out of the Father's hand. 30I and the Father are one." John 10:27-30

It was 3:00 am. My husband had been asleep for hours and my children even longer, but not me. I was just turning off the glow of my phone. My mind raced with all the chaos that was happening in our world. I should have known this would be a strange year when a young high school girl was murdered in her home just a little way from our home. I don't know of anything like that ever happening in my small country town. I knew I'd regret still being awake when morning came but here I was. There were so many sides to every current issue, and every one of them vehemently claimed to be true, and the other side was not just wrong but evil. I had friends I loved and respected on every side of every issue. It broke my heart to watch them tear each other apart. If they had been actually looking at each other face to face, I'm sure they would have said, oh, but you're the exception. Had I not seen that firsthand? Friends who encouraged us to get on food stamps would post things that shamed us and then say, oh, but you're the exception. No, I'm not, and your words cut deep. People are so much freer with their words on social media and easily swayed into seeing people as belonging to this group or that and never really seeing the people. Yet here I sit late into the night, reading and taking it all in, again. If I had been one of my kids, I would have taken away my phone and told them nothing should have control over them like that.

Far too early the next morning, I was up, and the first thing I did was to reach for my phone. It was my new habit, and it would be in my hands many times more until 2 or 3 am. With the way this world is going, anything could have happened in the last several minutes. One Saturday, I let the kids sleep and treasured the rare quiet morning. Since school had closed, all my kids were constantly underfoot. My husband's job sent him home, so he was constantly in my kitchen on zoom calls trying to work and getting frustrated if I made a sound. I couldn't even wash dishes because the water was too loud. And keeping the kids quiet...forget it. I kept reading things online about what you can do with your kids while we are all bored. I wasn't bored! I wanted my quiet back. There was no space for me, and I needed to cook more food than ever in a kitchen that was no longer mine. I was pretty sure I was near crazy. I didn't realize how much I needed space for myself or the many ways I had snuck it into our crazy life, but now my time and space always belonged to everyone else.

I took out my journal and began to write. I've had a journal since the early '80s. It was my diary, and I was going to be Laura Ingalls Wilder or maybe Anne Frank. Then I had children, and I began directing it to them and telling them of life even when they were still in the womb. But eventually, it became my journal to Jesus, and I would always start it with, "Dear Lord." We have wrestled through so many things over the years that I could write several books and have often been told I should. Maybe one day I will, but until then, I can tell you this, God is good, and God is faithful. Sometimes I am brought to tears when I look back and see the prayers of my heart and the way He has heard me and answered. Even though sometimes I was angry that His answer was, no or wait, looking back, it was good.

That day I wrestled with my recent obsession with social media. I wrote that I didn't understand what was happening. It was like I was seeking some post, some article, some comment that would make all the crazy make sense. Writing often helps me sort through and process my own thoughts, and that day was no different. I began to realize what I was doing, and instinctively, I knew the better answer as I wrote, "but the answers aren't on Facebook or Twitter, are they? They are only with You." I stopped writing as I let my new understanding sink in. I was looking for answers in all the wrong places. Frustration bubbled up inside my head, and I wrote, "But covid isn't in the Bible, and neither is race riots. There are no current events there. I need something for today." Don't worry, God didn't strike me with lightning. He is kind and patient, and He understands our struggles. I committed a long time ago to not fake how I feel with Him because He knows anyway, and it's only when I'm honest that we can sort through it all. Isn't that what the Psalms are? I closed my journal entry, determining to look at social media less and read my Bible more.

The next morning, we went to church just like we do every Sunday. Before going into his sermon, Pastor Cody gave us a free thought for the day. It was one that he didn't share in 1st service. He said, "Do you want to find peace in the midst of this crazy?" then he leaned on the podium, and half-joking, half-serious, he said, "Get rid of Facebook." Now before you stop reading and think I'm going to tell you Facebook is evil and that you need to get rid of all social media; no, that is not where I'm going. I will explain, but I'm telling you my story right now. For me, God answered in the audible voice of my pastor that morning. On my way home, I took Facebook off my phone and put the Bible app front and center. I turned my screen saver to quote Isaiah 26:3, *"You keep him in perfect peace whose mind is stayed on You, because he trusts in You."* That was over a year ago, and I don't miss it. The journey God has taken me on since then is so much better than the crazy I was facing. It was not easy, but good and peaceful. He keeps His promises.

I have a blog (mistysunshineblog.com) that I haven't really kept up, but it's still there, and I wrote a post in it on April 16, 2020, just before I gave up Facebook. I shared how I was wrestling with something that seemed as impossible as covid, and I shared how God led me to still waters, and even though I walked through the valley, I would fear no evil. At first, I saw His answer as cruel. He laid a phrase on my heart that came from the Bible, and I realized I didn't even actually know what it meant, but upon seeking it out, it brought even greater fear and seemed like a cruel joke. He didn't relent, and I pressed in seeking Him in the midst. It was there in the middle of my fears that He brought peace and clarity.

Dear Sheep,

We need to learn the voice of our Shepherd if we are going to survive. He will cause us to not simply survive but to thrive and know true eternal Life.

Often, we hear people talk about hearing from God, and we associate it with some kind of crazy hyper-spiritual thing. Or maybe it's just for the pastors. Or maybe we think it's an audible voice heard only once in a while by a few like Moses or Abraham. However, I would like to submit that that perspective is a lie of the enemy. Look at John 10:27-30 again and really read it. I know it's familiar and easy to brush over but read it again. If we are His sheep, we will hear His voice. That isn't only for a few or once in a lifetime. Many years ago, Philip Keller wrote a book called *"A Shepherd Looks at Psalm 23"* He helps us to understand the closeness that a shepherd has with his sheep. They cannot follow if he does not continually speak to them or, in turn, if they are not continually listening. It's probably why Paul encouraged us in *1 Thessalonians 5:17 to "pray without ceasing".* That doesn't mean talking constantly. Prayer is a conversation, not a monologue. It means to continually be attuned to what the Shepherd may be saying to us, where He may be directing us.

"Too many of us have exempted ourselves, believing that He doesn't talk to us lowly sheep, but in fact, that is exactly who it says He talks to."

AND He expects us to not only hear Him but to follow or obey His direction. To believe that He only speaks to the spiritual giants goes against everything the Bible teaches because it says He gives them eternal Life. If He only speaks to the rare few, then only the rare few can find eternal Life. That is NOT what John 3:16 tells us, "For God so loved the world, that He gave His only Son, that **whoever** believes in Him should not perish but have eternal life." Whoever is you and me! Whoever is whoever.

One of the most frightening verses in the Bible is Matthew 7:21-23, "21 *Not everyone who says to me, 'Lord, Lord,' will enter the kingdom of heaven, but the one who does the will of my Father who is in heaven. 22 On that day many will say to me, 'Lord, Lord, did we not prophesy in your name, and cast out demons in your name, and do many mighty works in your name?' 23 And then will I declare to them, 'I never knew you; depart from me, you workers of lawlessness.'"* However, Jesus tells us how to keep from hearing those dreadful words, "I never knew you." He tells us when we hear and follow; He knows us. God's name is powerful beyond anything we can imagine, and people apparently can use it for the power of it, and it will work because His name is great. He isn't seeking people who will use Him. He's seeking sheep who will know Him and hear Him and follow Him. How do we do that?

I certainly don't pretend to know all the answers. I am learning as I go, just like you, but I can tell you what I've learned over the years. I can tell you how I've been learning to know the voice of the Shepherd, and hopefully, if you already know, it will remind and encourage you to keep on keeping on. If this is all a little "out there" to you, let me share some of my stories so that you can begin to hear the Shepherd for yourself. So, you can follow, and we will all be together to celebrate for eternity the incredible things He will do.

There are many ways to hear the Shepherd. I will intermix different ways that He speaks with my stories of how I learned that. The most important one is often skipped over. Are you ready? It's by reading His Word, the Bible. I know it's confusing and boring and not relevant and blah blah blah blah blah. I've heard those very thoughts come out of my own mouth. As a child learning to read, I tried to read it on my own, and by the time I reached Exodus or Numbers, I checked out. I tried again, many times, and had the same result. So, I decided to just go to the New Testament, and immediately I was hit with a long, boring, meaningless genealogy. At least by chapter 2, a story was happening, but the writers were terribly vague, and it was difficult to really put a picture to the narrative. The characters were so lifeless and bland. What did they think? How did they feel? It didn't take long for other things to be far more interesting and draw my attention away until one day, I realized it had been weeks since I picked up my Bible. However, I knew it was important, so I tried again. This was my pattern for many years. I went to church and learned about His Word through my pastor, teachers, parents, and even radio preachers. I went to conferences, and I learned what many people said about what the Shepherd said, but I didn't really read it for myself.

In high school, I faced a crisis that shook my faith to the core. I became angry with God and decided He was not worth it. I started running from Him, and the path it took me down was dark. On the outside, I was still a great person and an example to many, but inside I was hurting like never before. I wrote in my journal that I wanted to die, and I felt awful. I formed a plan to carry out my wishes. A young man whom I wasn't even supposed to be talking to talked me out of it. Shortly after that, I finally relented and went to a youth group with a friend. A special speaker sang a song, and I was inclined to ignore it because he certainly didn't have a great voice. Maybe because it wasn't great to listen to, that the words leapt into my heart. The song that God gave to Wayne Watson was meant for me that day, and it came from a willing vessel with a not great voice. It was the voice of my Shepherd.

"Smile, make 'em think you're happy
Lie and say that things are fine
And hide that empty longing that you feel
Don't ever show it, just keep your heart concealed
Why are the days so lonely?
I wonder where, where can a heart go free
And who will dry the tears that no one's seen?
There must be someone to share your silent dreams
Caught like a leaf in the wind
Lookin' for a friend, where can you turn?
Whisper the words of a prayer, and you'll find Him there
Arms open wide, love in His eyes
Jesus, He meets you where you are
Jesus, He heals your secret scars

All the love you're longing for
Is Jesus, the friend of a wounded heart"...

It was too much. God had just spoken the very words I needed to hear through the song of a guy who couldn't carry a tune in a bucket, and I was ready to cry buckets. I went to the restroom to pull myself together. I couldn't let people see me like this. I was the strong one, the example...I washed my face and returned to my seat in time to hear him tell a story.

He said, "What if you were walking down the street and saw your best friend?" It was the loss of my best friend that had sent me spiraling into this crisis in the first place, so I was very keenly tuned in as he asked, "What would you do if they totally ignored you and walked away?". I knew what I would do. I would kill myself. Then he said, "How do you think Jesus feels when we do that to Him?". I didn't hear another word that night. The voice of my Shepherd was calling, and I had to obey. When I got home, alone in my room, I repented, and He welcomed me back.

With a new perspective, I began to read things in the Bible that I had never heard before. It was the same Bible, same words but alive and so relevant. We didn't have a youth group at our church, and my mom encouraged me to start one. I told her I was too young, and she told me to read 1 Timothy 4:12, *"Do not let anyone look down on you because you are young but set an example for the believers in speech, in life, in love, in faith and in purity."*. I started a youth group, and we all grew and learned.

Several years later, I was married to the man of my dreams, and we were expecting our first child, but life wasn't quite what we had dreamed. It was doing its best to turn into a nightmare. I was delivering papers with my big belly, and the weight of it all felt crushing. I was glad it was early morning so no one could see the tears that I couldn't stop. I told God I didn't trust Him, that He had let me down. The sound of the newspaper smacking the porch seemed to punctuate my new declaration. Then a thought, not my own, said, "Ok, whom or what will you trust?" I began thinking hard of an answer, and yet every single possibility had failed me in some way at some time. I knew they would again, not because they are cruel but because they are human. "Ok, fine," I said. "I'll trust You, but I don't know what to do." During the rest of my walk, an idea formed in my mind that seemed ridiculous. I told God that I would tell Marty (my husband), and if he agreed to such an absurd idea, we would take steps in that direction until the door closed. The door didn't close, and though it was rough, it was the answer that got us where we needed to be.

Later, I was a stay-at-home mom in a new neighborhood

(trailer park). My husband worked an average of 60-70 hours a week in 5 days. I was overwhelmed with loneliness and little ones who were in constant need. It was on my heart to make a meal for my neighbor, and I spent the day arguing that I didn't know her at all. What if she didn't even like what I made? I barely had money to feed my own family, but I finally relented and made enough to take some over to her and her husband. We became fast friends, and I was so glad I made that meal. God knew we both needed what the other had.

As time went on, our little family grew, and we did not fit in our little trailer. Marty and I began looking for a new place. One night after I had stayed up into the wee hours finishing the mound of laundry and putting it away, our oldest son Joshua got up in the night and stuffed all of the kids' clothes from their dressers into Meijer bags and piled them on the couch. The next morning, I was dumbfounded. He is terrified of the dark and a very obedient child. What on earth! He told me he had a dream that we were moving, and he wanted to make sure we didn't leave anything behind, so he started packing. He described the house to me, and it seemed as if it were just a ridiculous dream. No one puts a couch between their kitchen sink and table. In a series of events that only God could have orchestrated, we moved into a house where the layout of the kitchen, dining room, and living room was such that you could say the couch was between the sink and table.

On another occasion, one day, two hours from home with three kids in the car, I was loading stuff into the trunk. I had the keys in my hand, and they kept getting in the way. I set them aside in the trunk to finish loading. I told myself not to do that because I would forget they were there, but I argued with myself that I would not. It was only for a second. I did remember them - as my trunk slammed shut. My husband was not thrilled with coming to rescue me.

After coming home from church one evening, my husband could not find his keys. We searched the house for hours. I kept praying, God, please show us where the keys are, but the only thing in my mind was to look outside. Marty was absolutely convinced he brought them in, and one of the kids must have taken them. I opened the door to look outside in the dark. We found a toad on our step but no keys. I started asking God to please put them in the cupboard I was about to open, but He never did. Finally, we went to bed, and Marty went to work the next day. That day he needed to have others open things for him because his keys seemed to have vanished. Every time I prayed about it, I just kept thinking about looking outside. When Marty pulled in the driveway after work, I just started laughing so hard I could barely stand. The keys were outside alright. They were stuck in the roof rack of the car!

Another day, we had company, and my tiny kitchen didn't offer much counter space. I put the plastic dish drainer in the oven to make more room. I told myself not to do that but argued that nothing would happen, that the food was already made. When the guests arrived, one of them had brought garlic bread, so I preheated the oven. You guessed it. Smoke was billowing everywhere, and my drainer was, well, a puddle.

One day at church, I was waiting for my family to gather, and a young man was talking to some people near me. I couldn't hear their conversation, but I was struck with the question, 'When is someone going to do something about his immorality?'. I chided myself for having such a terrible thought about a leader I barely even knew, but I couldn't get it out of my head. I didn't dare speak it to anyone, but that evening we were told that he had come to the pastor about something immoral in his life and he would be stepping down from his position.

I often wondered, what was that? Why did I have to know that? Should I have done something about it? Over the years, as I have learned to hear the voice of my Shepherd more and more, I realize that He didn't tell me that information to do anything about it; He was taking care of it. I was only learning to know His voice. It comes through His Word, songs, people, dreams, thoughts, events, and more. He said in Luke 16:10, *"One who is faithful in a very little is also faithful in much, and one who is dishonest in a very little is also dishonest in much."*. I believe that He speaks to us in the little things so that we can learn to hear and know His voice. So then, when it comes to the big things, we will not hesitate but go forth in boldness because we know we heard the voice of our Shepherd.

We live in a day and age where there are so many voices constantly demanding our ear we must learn to tune in to the Shepherd or be lost. Even though I know my husband's voice, if we go to a crowded restaurant with loud music and noise, I cannot follow his conversation. It's not that I can't pick his voice out from a crowd, but I just can't hear it. For some of us, maybe we have been one of His sheep for a long time, and we know His voice well. However, if we constantly have noise on, it will be very hard to hear. Are we taking the time to listen? There is more noise than ever vying for our attention, and by next year there will be even more. We have to find a place to listen, or we won't be able to hear and obey.

We need to pick up our Bible and know that we know what it says. At first, we may not understand it, but over time we will learn. A baby in his mother's womb has no concept of the world outside, yet he learns to know and trust the voice of his mom. When he is born, she speaks tenderly to him, and he doesn't understand a word, but he knows that voice is safe. As he grows older, he begins to learn what those words mean and even how to obey them. Reading our Bible is a little like that. It is full of concepts we just don't understand, but we learn to trust it. We learn that voice, and little by little, we learn to understand and obey, and God, our gracious Heavenly Father, teaches us in the little things first: how to eat, how to walk, how to talk, and one day we will be mature in Him. But if we don't stick to hearing His Word, then how will we recognize it when He sends us a thought or a dream or a person or a song. We can be easily carried away by all manners of thoughts and eventually end up lost.

To go back where I started, whenever I found myself reaching for my phone, I had nothing to look at but my Bible. I started to listen to it every day when I drove home from work, and I have now listened through the whole thing multiple times, and guess what, every time I gain a little more. Some of it does still seem boring, BUT that's only because I haven't grown to that level yet. One day I will be listening, and all of a sudden, something I've heard a hundred times will suddenly come alive and change my life. For instance, as I was listening through the laws of the Old Testament, I couldn't wait for that part to be over. After all, Jesus came and fulfilled the law, and we aren't bound by it anymore. I got to Leviticus 5, and it was talking about when you make a foolish oath and how to make atonement for it or how to be set free from it, and I remembered a Bible story from Judges that has always bothered me. Judges 11:30-31, "*30And Jephthah made a vow to the Lord and said, "If you will give the Ammonites into my hand, 31then whatever comes out from the doors of my house to meet me when I return in peace from the Ammonites shall be the Lord's, and I will offer it up for a burnt offering."* The first thing out of his house was his only daughter! How does one reconcile this? Why did God let her come out first? I've heard multiple ideas on this passage, but if I know the whole Word of God, I know this. God had made a way of escape if Jephthah had known the Word, the voice of His shepherd. He did NOT have to keep his vow, and God never asks for such a thing. I started to realize that all those boring laws are God's incredible grace! He looked at our sin-filled lives and said, I know you will mess up. I know you will both make mistakes and even intentionally do things against what is good, but I am giving you a way to make it right. The laws aren't a list of dos and don'ts. They are God recognizing our fallen ways and giving us hope! That's why there are so many because we find so many ways to sin.

Another recent gem is when I was listening to the sections about the building of the temple. I could feel my eyes glazing over as I listened to this many cubits and this

material and this shape and this size...Then I remembered 1 Corinthians 6, *"do you not know that your body is a temple of the Holy Spirit.".* Wait a minute. If God puts that much care and detail into a temporary temple that He knows is going to be destroyed, does He put that much care into me? Does He really care about every detail and color and shape and size of my life? Yes, yes, He does!

He cares so much that He interrupts Pastor Cody's sermon to send me a message. He interrupts my son's sleep to send us a message. He interrupts my thoughts to send me a message. He sends a man who can't sing to sing words that I'll hear and a story that will save lives. He impresses things on our hearts and won't back down until we listen because He knows it's for our good. He even tells us silly little things like don't leave your keys in the trunk because He cares about even the little details. He tells us secrets meant for only us so that when the truth is revealed, we can know, I heard God's voice, and I am learning to know it.

Can I let you in on a little secret? He doesn't tell us all the same thing. What He tells each of us is customized for us. As we look around this crazy world and all that is happening, it is easy to say they should do this, or they should do that. We can look at what we are doing and wonder what's wrong with the other sheep? Why aren't they doing the same thing? But they are looking back and wondering the same thing about us. Paul gives us insight into that in I Corinthians 12 when he calls us the Body of Christ. Could you imagine the feet looking at the tongue and trying to imitate? I don't know about you, but I sure don't want to taste everywhere my feet walk. Or what if the heart decided to complain about how it has to work all the time while the legs often do nothing but hang off a chair. Maybe it should rest as much as the legs. If that happened, we wouldn't be alive to do anything. We have to stop looking around at everyone else and trying to imitate them or becoming jealous or angry or justified based on how we think the other sheep should act. The wise Shepherd leads each of us according to our need, our talents, our personalities. Maybe one sheep will wear a mask, and another won't. Maybe one will vaccinate, and another won't. Maybe one will protest, and another won't. Maybe one will stand up for truth while another will comfort in the shadows. Only the Good Shepherd knows exactly what is needed and who is needed for which job. The only way we can know what to do is to tune in to the Shepherd. Know His Word and take time to clear the noise so you can hear Him. It's the only way we will get through all the voices and noise of this world and know Life abundantly.

Misty is one of the Good Shepherd's sheep and wife to Marty. Together they have nine lambs. Five have grown, and four still live at home. She also works at WLMB TV40. More stories of Jesus in the midst can be found at mistysunshineblog.com.

Spiritual Axioms For Life 2022

As a young man, George Washington was greatly influenced by the book entitled "Rules of Civility and Decent Behavior in Company and Conversation." This book of 110 rules would help a young man know how to act like a gentleman throughout his life. This idea challenged me to write an ongoing list of spiritual truths that I have learned in life. Washington read his 110 rules to remind himself of what he wanted to become. I record them to remind myself of His truths so that I can live them out daily and represent Him well. Here are just a few Spiritual Axioms to consider:

Walking in faith does not mean that you avoid the trials of life.
Instead, it means that we learn how to overcome them.

Are you the mouthpiece for the world, or are you the mouthpiece for the Word

What you cannot see in the spiritual realm is greater than what you c
an see in the natural realm of this life.

Jesus said the Word is seed. Are you watering the seed with words
of faith or scorching it with words of doubt?

When you speak the Word in faith, your words are backed by the
thunderous voice of the Holy Spirit in the spiritual realm.

When you get truth from the Word, you have to put it into practice right
away for it to become part of your faith walk.

The mind that is operating in fear does not think clearly, rationally,
or even sanely. Fear distorts your thinking.

Service From 1st Corinthians

By Jeff Millslagle

The New Testament book of 1 Corinthians has been an emphasis of my personal study for quite some time. I have been curious about how the early church expanded and how the original readers of Paul's letters responded to his directives. While other books of his – notably Colossians and Philippians – are somewhat easier to dissect because of their length, both of his Corinthian letters share considerably more instruction. The length of those books, especially 1st Corinthians, makes line-by-line personal study a significant task.

There are plenty of commentaries and study guides available about the book, and opinions abound surrounding the modern application of this 2,000-year-old document. Therefore, it was not my goal to create another Corinthian study guide. I just wanted to see if there was a general theme within this book that I had previously overlooked.

As I started a slow verse-by-verse examination of 1st Corinthians, I expected I would learn some insights beyond what I already knew. What I began to see was something completely unexpected. Paul's answer to many of the issues facing the church revolved around service.

The church struggled to merge following Jesus into their culture. The society of 1st century Corinth was – on the surface – rather different than Jerusalem and Galilee. It wasn't the pharisees who were the main antagonists of Christianity but the Greek culture where philosophy and humanism were the arenas of battle for the church. They faced many issues. Division and disunity were chief issues within the church as one group thought they were of higher value because of who baptized them. They also faced a struggle as the educated held their status against those who were not as intellectual as they were. They allowed moral laxity for some – possibly because of wealth – and faced off against each other in civil courts. There was an arrogant presumption on the part of some because they chose to engage in liberties at the expense of others. Their exercise of spiritual gifts seemed to bring division within the body. These were just a few of the problems addressed by Paul.

The major lesson which struck me is one of service. There are no less than nine admonitions from Paul to the church about the idea of service. In each of their previously mentioned problems, one can see how Paul's answer to the situation was service. I believe understanding Paul's challenge to the Corinthian church about service is the key to understanding 1st Corinthians.

There are many parallels between the Corinthian church and our modern-day church. We, too, struggle with some of the same issues. I submit Paul's answer to the Corinthian church addressing their issues is applicable to us.

When we think of "service" or "serving in the church," we often tend to think about doing some task Sunday morning within the church building. Churches do need the help of volunteers, and depending on the church size or philosophy, there can be considerable places where serving is required. Greeters, parking lot attenders, children's ministry volunteers, tech teams, etc., are often major serving environments within a church. These are valid and meaningful areas of service, but I don't think this is the main thrust of Corinthians – just to get more people to serve coffee and operate a camera for the live feed.

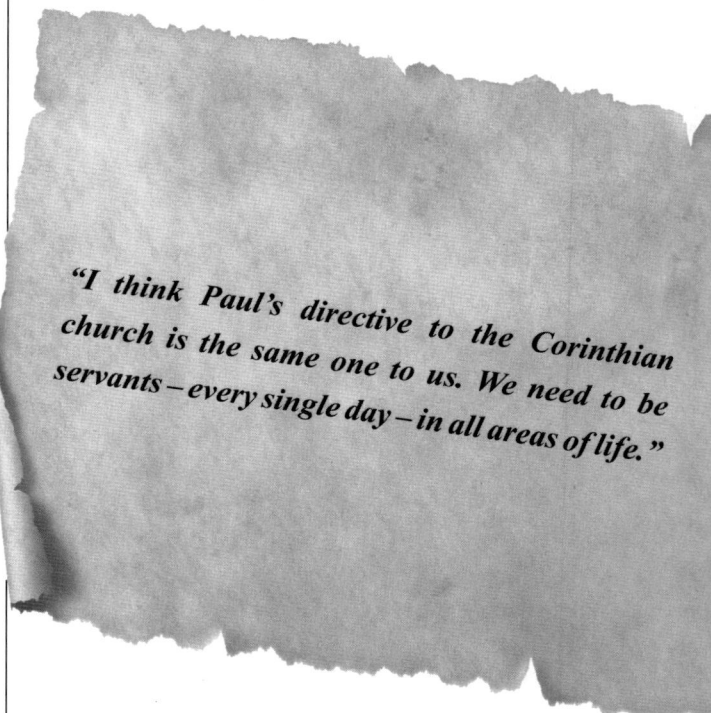

"I think Paul's directive to the Corinthian church is the same one to us. We need to be servants – every single day – in all areas of life."

With that introduction, let me point out these nine times I see Paul speaking of service

1. Service is Anonymous – 4:1-16

In the first 3 chapters of 1st Corinthians, Paul spent a significant amount of time addressing the idea of division within the church. Apparently, some felt they were more important Christians than others because of who had baptized them. The various factions competed with each other in a baptismal tug-of-war vying over spiritual supremacy. In chapter 2 the people were split down a line of intellectualism, and finally, Paul admonished them in chapter 3 by telling them to grow up! Their divisiveness was endangering their mission. He called them "babes in Christ" in verse 1 and how they were "still carnal" in verse 3.

He begins chapter 4 with a little-used word. He stated,

Let a man so consider us, as servants of Christ and stewards of the mysteries of God. – 1st Corinthians 4:1

The word we translate as "servants" in this passage is rather revealing. This is the only place it appears in any of Paul's letters. It is found predominately in Luke's writing and a few times in John's gospel. This is a different Greek word than we normally see used in the New Testament for "servant." The word refers to the oarsman of large Roman sailing vessels. The largest ships had two or even three levels of oarsman. This term describes those on the lowest level where the ship is the darkest as little natural light would make its way deep into the vessel. Those under-oarsmen were anonymous, thought of as slaves, and were also the most vulnerable. If the ship was damaged in any way and in danger of sinking, those oarsmen would be among the first to drown. The people of Corinth were familiar with those types of vessels.

Corinth was a city with a long history of the maritime industry. It was located on a narrow strip of land – an isthmus – between the mainland of Greece and the southern peninsula of Peloponnesus. Ships traveling between the Gulf of Corinth in the west and the Saronic Gulf in the east could make the long journey around the peninsula, and navigate the dangerous waters around Cape Malea. Or they could dock at Corinth, unload their vessels, and transport their cargo 6 miles across the isthmus, and reload it into waiting ships on the other side. Smaller vessels were dragged across the land bridge via a rail-like structure called a Diolkos.

Therefore, when Paul used this word, he was writing to them in terms they would fully understand. He called himself a servant, an under-oarsman, the lowest of the lowest servants. Additionally, he tells them in verse 16 to "imitate me." He expected his readers to follow his lead to be servants and not to be consumed with themselves.

We, too, must look to serve – in anonymous, unremarkable ways with little or no gratitude expressed by those whom we serve faithfully. We know full well, God sees our service. The results and recognition of our service are not up to us. Our service is to Him and to each other.

2. Service Is Being Willing To Lose – 6:1-7

The overt sexual sin within the Corinthian church, as described in chapter 5 tends to grab our attention, yet the problem of litigation between believers was just as catastrophic to the health of the body. Paul admonished the church for allowing this activity to continue. Slowly read the first three verses, and you can almost hear his voice rising as if he were speaking this passage. He builds in intensity with a series of questions. He then writes, "I say this to your shame." In verse 7 he called this action on their part "an utter failure." Paul was not kidding around on this idea.

Now therefore, it is already an utter failure for you that you go to law against one another. Why do you not rather accept wrong? Why do you not rather let yourselves be cheated? - 1st Corinthians 6:7

Evidently, those within the church body were so antagonistic with each other they resorted to the secular or "the unrighteous" to work out their issues. One presumes this practice was used more concerning civil as opposed to criminal matters.

We usually apply these verses with the blanket statement that believers should not take each other to court. While this is a correct application of the passage, I am more intrigued by the latter half of verse 7. "Why would you not rather accept wrong? Why do you not rather let yourselves be defrauded?"

While the word "servant" isn't used here, the idea of it is obvious. We are to willingly accept a solution to a disagreement – presumably where financial considerations are at stake – where we don't gain the upper hand. Looking out for and caring for others, putting them first before ourselves, laying down our rights, our claim, in preference to the claim of others is called service. It is putting someone else before ourselves.

But some might say, "Are we supposed to allow ourselves to be doormats, just let people take advantage of, abuse, and hurt us?" Let me be clear, no, we are NOT doormats, nor are we required to allow people to abuse us or take advantage of us. I don't think that's Paul's point at all.

The situation, as I understand it described, seems to be one of financial claims. When one party believed it had been wronged by another member of the Body, Paul wanted this to be worked out among each other. If both parties had the attitude of serving each other, if both were willing to suffer loss in deference to each other, this situation would be resolved without going to civil authorities. Both parties needed to have the attitude of putting the other first and had to be willing to accept wrong against themselves.

As I indicated earlier, I think this directive of Paul's and the application for us is when the conflict between believers is not criminal in nature. Of course, it is proper to take the necessary steps to protect yourself and your financial assets. In minor disagreements, wouldn't we all be better off if we'd just prefer each other? Step back, cease demanding our rights, and allow each other considerable latitude in conflicts. Get help from the church in settling matters if necessary, but remember, we are to serve each other.

3. Service Prefers Others Over Self-Liberty – 8:1-13

The explanation of this passage is rather straightforward as Paul confronted an issue of people eating food which had been originally offered to an idol. Paul's point was since an idol is nothing, then food offered to an idol is just food.

Yet I think we miss his summation of verse 13: *Therefore, if food makes my brother stumble, I will never again eat meat, lest I make my brother stumble.* – 1st Corinthians 8:13

Or in other words, I will not exercise a liberty if it offends another. My liberties are not the issue; the issue is the other believer.

Too often, our goal as Christians seems to be how far can we go before we cross a line and our action becomes sin. We want to push the limits concerning our own position but forget our actions – in this case, eating food previously offered to an idol – may offend another believer. In this case, when other believers who were offended by eating such food were present, Paul was saying, "Forget the meat, go grab a veggie burger."

Once again, it is the intentional act of putting others first. It was about serving them, in this situation, and not exercising a liberty.

Paul addresses this same issue in Galatians.

For you, brethren, have been called to liberty; only do not use liberty as an opportunity for the flesh, but through love serve one another. For all the law is fulfilled in one word, even in this: "You shall love your neighbor as yourself." - Galatians 5:13-14

We may exercise our liberty, but we must do so in a manner of preferring others. In Galatians 5, Paul said we are to "Walk in the Spirit and not fulfill the lust of the flesh"

(verse 16). If we are walking in the Spirit, then our liberties will not come before our love – our service – to others.

Understand, we do have freedom in Christ. We don't have a list of rules to follow, things we can't do, or activities we must perform. The law has been fulfilled by Jesus, and we, therefore, can walk in all His goodness. Yet this same liberty cannot be a license to sin, and it cannot be a weapon of pride and smugness used to flaunt our liberty.

Your liberty is not to supersede the responsibility we have to serve and prefer others. It is their comfort and convictions we are to honor before we indulge in liberties that we know others may find offensive. Others before self, it is the motto of a servant.

4. Service Adapts to Others – 9:19-22

Earlier in Chapter 9 Paul laid out his case of his right to claim certain privileges, namely accepting financial help. He evidently didn't take what he could have from the Corinthian church. He explained this further when he said,

For though I am free from all men, I have made myself a servant to all, that I might win the more - 1st Corinthians 9:19

Regarding both Jews and non-Jews, he worked to serve them. Even to those who were not within his normal sphere of influence, he became a servant, adapting his role to fit the group he was serving. His main goal was to win people to Jesus, and he expected to do his level best to be flexible enough to minister to (serve) anyone he could. Paul's example is service – to anyone on their terms! Rather than forcing someone to adapt to his customs, he was willing to serve within their framework.

Our role as modern followers of Jesus is to also maintain a degree of flexibility and learn to adapt to the culture in which we find ourselves. Instead of demanding others conform to our preferences and forcing them to change before we engage in any meaningful activity with them, we need to remain flexible in our service.

Many mission organizations understand this principle as they spend considerable time understanding the culture in which they serve. They know, if they can better relate to and understand the people, their message will be more likely to generate lasting fruit. Yes, they do share the gospel, but they also make it a major focus of their work to understand the society they are serving.

We must follow the example of Paul and learn to adapt our way of service and therefore become a bearer of good news to our culture, learning to serve them in ways they wish to be served. We must become "all things to all men" (verse 22).

5. Service is Choosing for Glory of God – 10:23-31

Paul addressed some further issues in Chapter 10. The first 13 verses were directed to avoid self-indulgence. Then beginning in verse 14 he discussed the idea of idol feasts and instructed people not to participate in those events. Even though the idol was nothing, some of those feasts were inviting demonic activity, and Paul said he did "not want you to have fellowship with demons" (verse 20).

He ties these ideas together when he states in verse 23 how "All things are lawful for me, but all things are not helpful." This idea came to a natural conclusion when he wrote,

Therefore, whether you eat or drink or whatever you do, do all to the glory of God. – 1st Corinthians 10:31

Notice, whatever we do, we are to do to God's glory… not to our glory or comfort or pleasure. Our service, everything we do is to God's glory. Our struggle is that too often, we compartmentalize our actions – and our lives – into our Christian life and our secular life. Some even think the two areas cannot or should not overlap. But of course, Paul has told us everything in our life must be done for the glory of God.

Your vocation, your choice of dishwasher, your vacation, how you mow your lawn, the list is endless. If we perform these tasks with a mindset of "how can I glorify God in this activity or decision," we are serving Him as Paul has directed?

As a follower of Christ, now we must put Jesus at the head of every decision. Therefore, when Paul says "all things are lawful," he is right. But he is also directing us to ask ourselves, "Is what I am doing glorifying Him – or am I bringing glory to myself?" Even a lawful activity may be done for one's own glory.

We are to serve our Lord every day, all day. It isn't just a Sunday thing. It's every day, every hour, minute by minute. Because we are servants, we must do everything to the glory of God.

A true servant of Jesus knows He has the ultimate authority and power over one's life. Everything we do as His servants is all for His glory. Everything must be done in alignment so that He gains the glory for our activity. I believe this also includes how we treat each other. If we are to serve Him, we are to serve each other. We do all for the glory of God.

6. Service Waits For Each Other – 11:33

Chapter 11 of 1st Corinthians addressed two major issues. The first issue is covered in the first 16 verses. This is the instruction regarding women and head coverings. While there are a small number of church groups (i.e., German Baptist, Old Order Mennonite, and Amish) who place considerable emphasis on these verses, most churches – whether Catholic or protestant – no longer find modern application in this passage.

I am not attempting to explain those opening verses as I do not fully grasp Paul's intention. The covering of the female head is not discussed in any other of Paul's writing, nor do you see this demonstrated in the Book of Acts. It would seem only this church at Corinth was given this mandate.

However, the second concern begins in verse 17 as Paul spent the balance of the chapter addressing communion. In contrast to the first 16 verses, most modern churches take considerable application from this second half of 1 Corinthians 11.

Evidently, one group of believers used the communion meal as some sort of status symbol. One group would come to the gathering with large quantities of food for their own consumption. Then, they proudly engaged in a meal while another group of those who "have nothing" (vs. 22) were unable to bring much and therefore were publicly shamed because of their poverty.

Paul's language is rather strong on this matter. "I do not praise you" in verse 17 and again in verse 22. The celebration of communion is to be a church-wide event. It isn't a place to brag about one's social status or display culinary talents. It is meant to be a singular event to commemorate His death for our sin. To dilute the LORD's Supper is a grievous sin of significant proportion. In this act of communion, we see how each of us, deserving death, is saved by His voluntary redemptive sacrifice.

The Corinthian church had twisted this solemn event and turned its focus onto themselves. Therefore, when Paul came to the end of his communion instruction, he concluded it with the phrase, "When you come together to eat, wait for each other" (verse 33). Give preference to each other. See to it all are served. Make this about Him and not about you.

Here is where I revisit the early section of this chapter. If one applies Paul's instructions in our modern culture, I think it must center on service. Serving others is the overall theme, and for some, it may take a visual reminder to be a servant. It is possible that the covering served as this visual reminder of service, and its use isn't nearly as important as the lesson it portrayed. Like communion, we are to look out for, wait on, and serve others. It must be others first before self.

7. Service Generates Unity – 12:25

The book of 1st Corinthians addresses many issues prevalent in this early church. One substantial problem was the exercise of spiritual gifts. Those gifts are the topic of this chapter. After Paul's instruction about spiritual gifts and their use, his argument built to a crescendo in verse 25. He said,

...there should be no schism in the body but that the members should have the same care for one another. – 1st Corinthians 12:25

The term he uses for "schism" means to tear or rip apart. Paul did not want there to be divisions within the church.

Earlier in this chapter, Paul taught how each individual brought unique gifts to the church body, and each person had a different role. All of those gifts and roles were necessary. Keeping with his human body metaphor comparing it to the church body, he said the foot cannot think less of itself because it is not a hand (verse 15). It is the same with the ear and eyes (verse 16). Clearly, Paul was acknowledging different gifts upon individuals. At the same time, he did not wish to see the church ripped or torn apart because of individual gifts and roles.

We are to allow for and welcome our diversity because understanding these differences makes a unified body. Each part – each member – knows the importance of each other. This isn't an effort to make everyone the same. We are all different, diverse, but we can be unified when we accept and appreciate our different roles.

Service is the key to grasping this chapter. Just as mentioned previously, "servant" and "service" are not stated directly, yet it is plain to see where understanding and allowing differences in roles or gifting betters the whole body. We serve each other when one role or gift is not elevated above another. Where diversity is welcomed, recognized, and encouraged, unity – not 'sameness' – flourishes.

The result of this understanding is "...the members should have the same care for one another" (verse 25b). If one member suffers, all the members suffer, and the same is true if one member is honored. We are to suffer together and rejoice together. We are one body with different gifts, serving each other.

Looking out for others, preferring others before self, and not considering one person of greater value to the body because of their unique gift was Paul's point. The gifts are not to be used as weapons but are to be used in service to each other; others first before self, serving others before highlighting your gifts. Recognizing, allowing for, and encouraging differences actually creates unity.

Paul wasn't speaking against the use of any gift, but he was instructing the Corinthian church – and we who read his words 2,000 years later – that all gifts were to be centered around service to the body, not selfishly applied to meet some needed affirmation in ourselves, but to meet the needs of others.

"We are more enlightened than you are," should never be the mantra of a church body. We should never arrogantly promote our special role but look for opportunities to serve His church with our diverse gifts.

8. Service is Demonstrated by Love – The Entirety of Chapter 13

The quick transition from spiritual gifts to possibly the greatest discourse ever written on love takes place from verse 31 of chapter 12 where Paul says, "I will show you a more excellent way."

Chapter 13 is often a featured part of wedding ceremonies. While, of course, it fits within the marriage discourse, do not limit your understanding or application of this chapter to just a couple's nuptials. Marriage isn't mentioned in this passage. It is too narrow an application of this chapter to limit it to marriage. This is more than a wedding charge; it is a manual for all of us to follow within the Body of Christ.

Beginning in verse 1 of chapter 13, he made the bold statement showing how love has a greater value than the gift of tongues. Prophecy is of no match to love (verse 2), and even a gift of giving or martyrdom is still of no value apart from love (verse 3).

Paul is teaching how love suffers long, is kind, does not parade itself (verse 4), love does not seek its own (verse 5), and the list continues. These are all descriptions of serving. This is how a servant is supposed to conduct themselves, looking out for and serving each other in love.

The first seven verses do not mention anything about how the individual operating in this manner is lifted up or elevated in status. Rather, all of these actions prefer others over self. Love, as seen in service to others, is to be our prime motivator.

Possibly, servanthood is the tell-tale evidence of the depth of our love as selfishness has no room in this chapter.

Allowing for only expressions of servanthood, this chapter is a clinic on how we must relate to each other. Love, as expressed in service, is the yardstick of discipleship. If you are a true follower of Jesus, your ability to serve others – with no selfish motivation or expectation of a returned act of service – is the identifying mark of a true Christ-follower.

Often the church finds itself demanding our rights. We have the right to assemble. We have the right to worship as we please, to say what we want to say, etc. Those, of course, are true statements as our right to assemble, our freedom of worship, and freedom of speech are all sacrosanct under the US Constitution. As US citizens, we function under various governing bodies. However, within the broader context of our heavenly citizenship, we have a different and higher authority we must submit to. Our assembly, our worship, our actions are all governed, not by a ruling class or civil authorities, but by His Word. His Word invites us to function as servants.

Servants can demand nothing. Servants serve their masters out of fear or obligation. However, we serve our Master out of love. Demanding our rights elevates ourselves, while service to God elevates others. How we conduct ourselves, how we love others, is how we serve. As servants, we do not demand, but we serve.

9. Service is Devotion – 16:15

As Paul wrapped up his lengthy letter, he stated his desire to visit the church and closed with some personal greetings. One of those individuals he mentioned is Stephanas. Paul writes,

I urge you brethren – you know the household of Stephanas that it is the firstfruits of Achaia, and that they have devoted themselves to the ministry of the saints. - 1st Corinthians 16:15

We are given few details about Stephanas, but we do know his service was not just limited to only himself. As stated by Paul, the household of Stephanas engaged in many acts of service. He must have been an early convert of Paul's and quickly became a place of encouragement to the Body of Christ. Paul referred to them as "devoted" to ministry. They evidently were aware of various needs and made it a point to serve others. What all they did, we really don't know as we are left to speculate about what form their service or "devotion" took.

The description of the household of Stephanas is interesting to me. First, it was a family thing. This isn't just an individual serving, but the entire family picked up the servant mantel.

Second, they "devoted themselves" or made a commitment. The word used for devoted means "to arrange in an orderly manner." This wasn't just a few random acts on the part of him and his family, but it was a well-thought out, orderly plan. They made it their goal to minister or serve others, in particular those within the church.

Finally, as a result of their service, they had some spiritual authority. Paul tells the Corinthian church to submit to them and possibly those like them (verse 16). The orderly manner in which they served others needed to be exercised in the church body as it is likely the Corinthian church struggled with order.

The household of Stephanas is a serving model for us – not of what they did – but for their orderly manner of how they served. It was an intentional decision of making a point to serve the church.

I am sure these nine instances of serving or servanthood are not the only examples of service within 1st Corinthians, but these nine have jumped out at me. While I haven't heard or read much about how service is a major theme of this book, to my way of understanding, every issue within the book of 1st Corinthians can be addressed by understanding and applying this principle; we are to be servants of God and of each other.

The Greek and Roman cultures of the 1st century were very self-centered. The early church struggled with mixing accepted cultural norms into their gatherings and too often made "self" their center. Other people, particularly the poor or those of lower social status, were taken advantage of by the wealthy. Paul's admonition to them was the church must rise above the moral decay around them and must look out for and serve all people.

I wonder if all the often-mentioned problems within the Corinthian church were all indicators of the main issue – a lack of service to each other. I believe this is the biggest problem in our modern church as we struggle with the entire idea of servanthood. We tend to focus on symptoms and rarely address the main issue.

The situation in 1st century Corinth did not look very different than our North American culture. Wealth, status, and personal comfort, all reign supreme in our world. The unintended consequence of unbridled prosperity for many has been an avalanche of needs for others.

Therefore, it is imperative we look for lessons of service from 1st Corinthians. We look beyond just the obvious surface problems they experienced. We must take Paul's message to heart and learn to serve. We need to be as the household of Stephanas and devote ourselves and arrange in an intentional orderly manner, to the service of others.

In two places, Paul tells the Corinthian church to "imitate me." In chapter 4:16 and again in 11:1. Those words are also directed to us. We are to imitate Paul, the "under-oarsman" and servant of all. If, in fact, more of us in the church looked to the care of others, unselfishly served others, and put others first before ourselves, wouldn't the struggles within our churches subside?

The problems of disunity, social unrest, injustice, and selfishness might all be addressed by the church taking our cue from Paul, learning to put others first and serve one another.

Jeff Millslagle is the Program Director at WLMB TV-40 in Toledo. Jeff has been a student of the Scriptures for nearly 40 years and has a deep passion for presenting the Word of God in a variety of forms. Jeff and his wife Orpha have been married 42 years and live in the Toledo area.

Do You Know Your Position

By Donna Hostetler

When we are born into this world, it is a physical birth. We are physically placed into a home without our consent. It could be a good home with two loving parents. It could be a broken home with only one parent, poverty, dysfunction, or hate. Perhaps we were not wanted, or our mother could not care for us, and we were put up for adoption or raised "in the system." Regardless, we inherit whatever physical situation we find ourselves in. Our thinking, perspectives, wants, desires, hopes all come from whatever physical position we were put in. That affects our opinions, viewpoints, worldview, and how we see our Heavenly Father. It is a position that we didn't choose. We were physically brought into this carnal world.

When we become born again, we <u>choose</u> to be spiritually born. It is a spiritual choice. We choose to accept God's precious gift of His Son and the sacrifice He made for us. We accept that He loves us so much that He gives us a chance to step into a glorious life. When Jesus died on the cross and shed His blood for us, He positioned everyone that accepts Him into His spiritual Kingdom. It is now our choice to move into our spiritual position. When we say yes to Him, we get all of the benefits of being a child of God. It is a spiritual birth. And it is our choice. Because of our choice, we inherit all of God's best. Now the Holy Spirit can come in and affect our opinions, viewpoints, worldview, and most significantly, how we see our Heavenly Father.

Now that we are born "again," this choice we make brings us into eternal life, the life that our Heavenly Father wanted for us all along. It allows us to move beyond the sin we inherited from Adam. No longer are we chained by the curse and death, but we are free to move into the high spiritual realm of life in Jesus. We are now the righteousness of Christ which positions us above all who won't or haven't yet made the choice to be born again. They are living only in the position of their natural physical birth.

I am quoting this directly because it is too good to try to summarize!

"'When God came into the garden of Eden after the fall of the first man, the Bible says: "But, the Lord God called to the man, *"Where are you?"'"* Genesis 3:9 NIV

This question – *"where are you?"* from God to Adam had nothing to do with his physical position or location in the garden. It had everything to do with his spiritual position and location, in exercising spiritual authority in the garden over all of God's creatures, including the serpent. Adam was not standing in his position of spiritual authority when God came looking for him in that position." *Bible Vision International Ministries.*

Adam gave up his spiritual position, but our wonderful Heavenly Father already had a plan in place to give us the opportunity to get it back! We have a way to move from just a physical position in this carnal world to a spiritual position through Jesus Christ. Our spiritual birth puts us back into "The" family of God. We are now spiritually positioned as a child of God. Merriam Webster's Dictionary tells us that position is a "relative place, situation, or standing; a situation that confers advantage or preference." What does that mean for us? As a child of the Most High God, we have received all the rights and privileges that He has given to His son, Jesus. We are immediately adopted into His home, His Kingdom. All that sounds wonderful! However, we are responsible for learning how to hold our position, be a child of the Most High God, and represent our Heavenly Father.

The first thought that came to my mind when I thought about how miraculous it was that we could choose to be Father God's child [spiritually] is, "How do I fit in?" If you were adopted in this natural world, you would be moving in with people you either didn't know or didn't know well. And you would then be subject to their household rules, traditions, interactions, and lifestyle. As their newest child, you would be expected to represent their family because you were now a part of that family. How you carry yourself, how you interact with people, how you conduct yourself, and how you fit in would all reflect on your new adoptive parents. It is more than a legal standing that you now have with the family. Your attitudes and behaviors need to mature, perhaps change, or cease depending upon your past behavior.

Likewise, as part of the family of God, we need to present ourselves, conduct ourselves in ways that reflect our new position. It is more than just having a spiritual legal standing through Christ. We must now learn who we are in Christ, what our position is in the Kingdom of God, and above all, how to reflect all that the Heavenly Father has given to us and called us to do.

We can no longer look at ourselves the way our physical family, friends, co-workers, employers, etc., see us. Until we see ourselves through the lens of God, we can't fill our position well. How does God see us? Through His Son.

So, Jesus is the key. Now we have to shift our mindset from "what I must do" to "what He has done." We have to rise above our old thinking and how we approach things. It's not unlike being hired into a position with a company. You have a job description, qualification requirements, expectations, and a supervisor. Jesus already "qualified" us, so we are in! Now we need to understand our new position and what's expected. The best part is that, unlike a physical job, we have the Holy Spirit alongside us at all times; coaching, directing, teaching, leading, and inspiring us. However, we still must do our part; we must understand the position!

There has been much written about who we are in Christ. Here are just a few things that explain who we are:

- Sons and Daughters
- Right Standing
- Ambassadors
- Disciples
- Students
- Soldiers/warriors
- Teachers
- Intercessors
- Prophets
- Hands and Feet
- Friends of God
- Abraham's Seed
- Kings & Priests

That's a lot of descriptions! Each is worthy of further study. We are all of these things and more. But just like any new position, we need to learn the basics before we can grow into the full scope of the position. The Holy Spirit is a patient and faithful teacher. Expect for this to take your lifetime to grow and expand into all of the positions you hold in the born again life.

As we grow in our relationship with our Heavenly Father, the more we understand what we are to do. The more we practice doing what our positions in Christ require of us, the more we are confident in who we are and what our authority is. It is not unlike the role of an earthly boss toward his employees. A good boss has more responsibilities than simply hiring new employees. That is just the beginning. Once the people are hired, they must be trained. A good boss knows that the people in his employ will have to first learn the job in order to expand and do more. A good boss understands his responsibilities toward those who work for him.

Do the employees have all the tools they need? Do they receive encouragement and feedback so they can grow? And, above all, is the environment or atmosphere one that allows them to learn from their mistakes without punishment so they can become a better worker?

The best part of being in the position of a child of God is that no matter what, we have all that we need, and we are always seen through the lens of Christ. He is perfect! When God looks at us, He sees Christ so that our mistakes, our shortcomings, our imperfections are not seen. If God doesn't see them, why do we keep looking at them? He designed our position from the very beginning of time. And He wants us to enjoy our position with confidence and trust in Him! All that we see Jesus has, we also have. If we have the full backing of the King of Kings, then we need to understand that we also have His authority. We have His provision, His wisdom, His protection, His support, His constant presence through the Holy Spirit. As He is, so are we in the world.

Our new spiritual position brings with it responsibilities, just like a physical job does. When I was in management and supervising people, I often had to remind people to just do their job. Too often, people were focused on what others were doing or not doing, what they perceived as unfair, or people who weren't "doing it right," and not on what they were responsible for. Countless times I would say, "Just do your job. Don't worry about anyone else. If you do your job, and do it well, that is all that is required of you".

The same is true in your spiritual position. Know what your spiritual position is. Know what your spiritual job is and do it. Don't worry about others, what they are called to do, how well they are doing it, or how "cool" their job might be. We each are called to a specific spiritual position in the body of Christ. The only person's opinion we need to be concerned with is the opinion of Christ. If He is pleased with what I am doing in my spiritual position within the Kingdom of God, then that is all that matters. Just as Jesus said to Peter when he asked what about the Apostle John after his resurrection: *"Peter, seeing him, said to Jesus, "But Lord, what about this man? 22Jesus said to him, "If I will that he remain till I come, what is that to you? You follow Me."* John 21:21-22, so we are just to keep our eyes on Jesus. Follow Him, and He will take care of the others around you.

Understanding our spiritual position requires our time to be focused on our Father. How else can we learn what the family is all about if we don't know what the head of the household wants? How can we emulate our Father if we don't know anything about Him? He's the best of the best! We need to allow the Holy Spirit to flow through us so that we can reflect Him to others because we represent the best. As we grow in our position, we need to be seeking insight into what gifts He has given to us. *"I will praise you for I am fearfully and wonderfully made;"* Psalm 139:14. We were designed by Him from before we were born. That means we were born with the gifts and callings He has placed in each of us. Over our lifetime, we discover what they are and develop them so that we can exercise the authority of our position. But often, we sabotage ourselves!

For example, if you feel that God has called to you sing, but you know that there are others who sing much better than you, it doesn't take away from the fact that God has placed singing in your heart. Instead of comparing ourselves to others and what they can do or are doing, we need to look at what God has asked us to do. To do otherwise can cause us to just not do it. Our insecurities can sabotage us. You don't have to be better than someone else or, in this case, a perfect singer. If God called you to sing – sing to Him. If He chooses to have you also do more, He will promote you. In the meantime, just sing to Him with all that He has given to you. As in the garden before the fall, He just wants our fellowship. In this example, you singing to Him.

As I look over the list of positions that we have spiritually once we are born again, which I presented earlier, there are two that I would like to address. The first is Abraham's seed. Even though Abraham is "Old Testament," he lived before the law. And He was blessed by God. *"And if you are Christ's, then you are Abraham's seed, and heirs according to the promise."* Galatians 3:29 Abraham was certainly not a perfect man. He waited many, many years to have a son. Mistakes were made while waiting for God's promise [Ishmael for one]. We can learn much from the life of Abraham and how God called him" friend." Friend means "- a person who you like and enjoy being with - a person who helps or supports someone or something." While Abraham had a relationship with God, I think God also enjoyed being with Abraham. Mistakes and all, Abraham followed what God asked him to do. It may have taken him a while, but he obeyed and was greatly rewarded.

We still can see God's promise to Abraham that he would be a father to many nations, *"Look now toward heaven, and count the stars if you are able to number them." And He said to him, "So shall your descendants be."* Genesis 15:5. Today, even though our modern-day skies are full of ambient light, you can still see many, many stars on a clear night and be reminded that if God fulfilled His promise to Abraham, how much more will He do that for you because of who you are in Christ?

Being a part of Abraham's inheritance means that all of the promises God made to Abraham [See Deuteronomy 28:1-14, for example] are ours today because we are part of the seed of Abraham. Our spiritual position includes the inheritance of God's promises. It is an inheritance that we receive because we have chosen Jesus. The best part is that there is enough inheritance for everyone who is spiritually born into the family. It is an inheritance that no one can take or challenge, and this spiritual position puts us into our Heavenly home. How awesome is that? Just as we prepare space in our earthly homes for the coming of a new member of the family, how much more does God prepare a place and provision for us in our spiritual home.

The second position we have is as an ambassador. Again, turning to the dictionary, ambassador means: "an official envoy *especially:* a diplomatic agent of the highest rank accredited to a foreign government or sovereign as the resident representative of his or her own government or sovereign or appointed for a special and often temporary diplomatic assignment"; "an authorized representative or messenger." This earthly world is the "foreign government," run by Satan. We are now ambassadors for Christ here in this fallen world. While we may feel more secure in who we are in Christ and are learning more and more about what is expected from us in our position, we still have to live in this physical world until Jesus' return! I have some final thoughts on what we need to remember and a few more aspects of our position as born-again believers. There is an ongoing battle between the physical and spiritual worlds. Now that we are in a spiritual position, we must use all of the weapons and tools of the spiritual world as we stay in this world as ambassadors for Christ.

How we feel physically can often affect our spiritual position. It takes our focus off our place in the Kingdom, and instead, we are focused on physical things. The enemy uses sickness and other physical and mental attacks to distract us. When this happens, we must saturate ourselves with the Word to get back into the "correct" position. More time must be spent in/on our spiritual life than our physical life. We must use our weapons of praise, the power of the spoken Word [speaking the Word out loud, speaking directly to the mountains in our path], and our direct line to our Heavenly Father through the Holy Spirit that is in us. Remember that our spiritual position is also how we see ourselves vs. how God sees us when we are in the spiritual world. The enemy sees you as you are in the spiritual world when you are operating in the spiritual. He sees you when you are operating in/from a physical perspective. He is terrified of you when he sees you in the spiritual realm. His words of deceit and destruction can't affect you in the spiritual realm.

What do we look like in the spiritual realm? *"Then I looked, and there was a likeness, like the appearance of fire—from the appearance of His waist and downward, fire; and from His waist and upward, like the appearance of brightness, like the color of amber."* Ezekiel 8:2. This is Jesus, and because we are in Jesus, this is the way we look in the spiritual realm.

When we follow the Word of God, our enemy sees us *"strong in the Lord and in the power of His might. [11]Put on the whole armor of God, that you may be able to stand against the wiles of the devil. [12]For we do not wrestle against flesh and blood, but against principalities, against powers, against the rulers of [b]the darkness of this age, against spiritual hostsof wickedness in the heavenly places. [13]Therefore take up the whole armor of God, that you may be able to withstand in the evil day, and having done all, to stand".* Ephesians 6:10-13

We must stay in our spiritual position to keep our thoughts from being deceived and our hearts from being turned. We must use our spiritual weapons to turn away the enemy and chase him down! Remember, the best weapon we have is "it is written." When you see lies or deceptions coming at you, just quote God's Word, and he must flee! It is part of your authority in your spiritual position. *"'**No weapon** formed against you shall prosper, And every tongue which rises against you in judgment You shall condemn. This is the heritage of the servants of the Lord, And their righteousness is from Me,' Says the Lord."* Isaiah 57:14. Your Father has your back! And He has given you His authority to use. Will you use it?

It is exciting to be in a spiritual position, in the family of God, representing Him in this world as His ambassadors. Learn all that you can about who you are in Christ. Exercise those weapons of intercession, praise, prayer, supplication, and the spoken Word. This year is going to be a pivotal one for the world and for the believer. It is crucial that everyone know his spiritual position and stand in that position. We must show the world that the only way is to choose to leave their physical position so that they can join us in our spiritual position. It is the Father's design of the new birth.

Credits

1. Bible Vision International Ministries; "Are you Standing in our position of spiritual authority." biblevisionintministries.org

2. Andrew Wommack; Andrew Wommack Ministries

3. Ward Cushman; To Every Nation Ministries;

4. Iain Gordon; Cru "How to Know your Position on Christ"

5. Merriam-Webster Dictionary

A believer for most of her life, Donna retired from a 30+ year career in management and administration to be in full-time ministry. Married to Todd Hostetler for more than 39 years, she is now the administrator for City on a Hill Teaching Center.